The British Museum

GODDESS

DR JANINA RAMIREZ ♦ **SARAH WALSH**

To Dan, Kuba and Kama . . .
And particularly, original goddess of inspiration – my mother, Danusia.

J. R.

To all the magical and unique beings in my life. You bring so much strength,
humour, love, understanding and magic to my world just by being yourselves.
And I'm forever grateful for it.

S. W.

First published 2022 by Nosy Crow Ltd
The Crow's Nest, 14 Baden Place,
Crosby Row, London, SE1 1YW, UK

Nosy Crow Eireann Ltd
44 Orchard Grove, Kenmare,
Co Kerry, V93 FY22, Ireland

www.nosycrow.com

ISBN 978 1 78800 995 9

Nosy Crow and associated logos are trademarks
and/or registered trademarks of Nosy Crow Ltd.

Published in collaboration with the British Museum.

Text © Dr Janina Ramirez 2022
Illustrations © Sarah Walsh 2022

All photographs © The Trustees of the British Museum 2022
(Except pages 12, 25, 29, 33, 42, 47, 54, 80, 91, 93, 105, 107 – see page 112 for credits)

The right of Janina Ramirez to be identified as the author and Sarah Walsh
to be identified as the illustrator of this work has been asserted.

A CIP catalogue record for this book is available from the British Library.

Printed in China.

Papers used by Nosy Crow are made from wood grown in sustainable forests.

3 5 7 9 8 6 4 2

The British Museum

nosy crow

GODDESS

50 GODDESSES, SPIRITS, SAINTS
AND OTHER FEMALE FIGURES WHO HAVE SHAPED BELIEF

DR JANINA RAMIREZ ◆ SARAH WALSH

CONTENTS

LOVE AND WISDOM

ANIMALS AND NATURE

INTRODUCTION

" Listen to your inner goddess."
" You look like a goddess in that dress! "
"Beyoncé is a total goddess."

The word *goddess* gets used a lot, often to compliment a woman on her beauty, her strength of character or her individuality. Unlike in the past, when we use the word today it is not necessarily connected to spirituality or belief. Traditionally goddesses reflect every possible human characteristic – some are beautiful, many are strong and all are individual. But the most important thing is that they are not just of this world – they exist almost as timeless beings. They entrance and empower people across time and space and their stories tap into the needs, desires, fears and hopes inside all of us.

Some of the figures in this book are not actually known as goddesses by the people that honour them. So Mami Wata is a spirit, Mary is a saint, Rangda is a demon, Baba Yaga is a witch and Pele is a mountain. It is important to see the differences between these figures and the people that value them, as they reveal the many varied views of individuals, communities and cultures. It would be impossible to include all the different belief systems around the world as there are a staggering number of inspirational females bringing hope and help to people all over the globe.

Reading about these figures will not only open your eyes to fascinating stories that are so compelling, exciting and intriguing that humans have been passing them on for hundreds, even thousands, of years. It will also show you the world in all its complexity and beauty. With Popa Medaw you can travel to the fragrant mountains of Myanmar (also known as Burma). Durga takes you to the bustling banks of Indian rivers during heady festivals, while Itzpapalotl transports you to the Aztec temples and dense jungles of Mesoamerica.

You might think a goddess needs to be beautiful, perfect and pure. But the classical image of a partly dressed, 'perfect' female, so common from ancient Greek and Roman sculptures, simply does not fit outside European cultures. And the goddesses in this book are so much more than that. Some are creators, birthing all life and representing a mother's love for her children. Others are leaders, full of wisdom and knowledge, guiding and protecting kings and queens as they rule on earth. Some are terrifying in their bloodthirsty strength, able to dominate the battlefield and destroy their enemies. And others are magical, mystical, mysterious figures who can control time, change fate and spin destiny. Each one can inspire you in different ways.

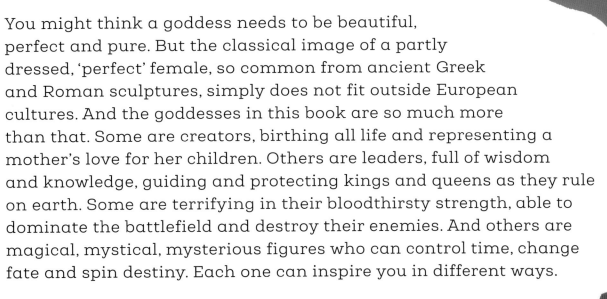

Perhaps there is a 'goddess' in all of us, because their stories reflect every aspect of what it means to be alive. These female figures show us that we too have the ability to be inspiring and powerful. Sometimes we can be strong, sometimes we can be peaceful, sometimes we can be loving, sometimes we can be vengeful. The women of the past were no different from us today in these basic ways and understanding them can help us to understand ourselves better.

Which one of these inspiring figures speaks to you and why? Ask yourself that as you travel the world through these remarkable stories. In today's world we don't have a single definition of femininity, beauty and the role of women. In these stories even the notions of male and female are fluid, so the endlessly transforming, shape-shifting figures reflect aspects of ourselves. They're not perfect, but they're fascinating. They're not one-dimensional, but complex.

The goddesses, spirits, saints and other female figures in this book have shaped belief over millennia and their stories deserve to be told.

INANNA

Mesopotamian Goddess of Love and War

QUEEN OF CONTRADICTIONS

Inanna was one of the greatest goddesses in ancient Mesopotamia: terrifying, confident, glorious and fickle. As a goddess of both love and war, the chaos of nature and the power of rulers, she was unpredictable. If she chose to love and protect you, you would feel joy and passion. If she disliked you, she could utterly destroy you. Inanna is also known as Ishtar – two names for the same goddess. Inanna was used in Sumeria while Ishtar was used in Assyria and Babylonia, which were ancient civilisations that ruled around modern-day Iraq, Iran and Turkey from roughly 3500 to 1500 BC.

One of the most famous myths about Inanna shows just how easily her moods could change. The tale of the Bull of Heaven begins with the goddess trying to seduce the brave hero Gilgamesh. But Gilgamesh couldn't be charmed, and his rejection sent Inanna into a furious rage. She asked her father Anu, god of the sky, to help her get revenge.

She wanted to use his dangerous bull to attack Gilgamesh and said that if he didn't let her, she would smash the gates of the Underworld to pieces, releasing the dead so they could feed on the living. Anu warned that setting the beast free would bring seven years of famine to the people, but Inanna fiercely insisted she had enough food for everyone. She would not rest until he did as she said.

A clay mould of Inanna, Iraq, 2000–1750 BC

Anu reluctantly gave in and released the fearsome bull on to the people. It destroyed everything in its path, killing 100 men with just one fuming breath. The heroes Gilgamesh and Enkidu battled to destroy it – one grabbed the creature by the tail, the other drove a sword through its throat. Eventually, they managed to kill the bull and save the day, but the gods decided that one of the young heroes must die as punishment for slaying the mythical beast. Enkidu was chosen, leaving Gilgamesh to mourn for his friend for the rest of his life. So, through Gilgamesh's suffering, Inanna finally got her revenge.

THE GATES OF HELL

In one of the world's oldest poems, the goddess goes to the kingdom of her sister, Ereshkigal, Queen of the Dead. When Inanna arrived at the Underworld, dressed in beautiful gowns as Queen of Heaven, her sister was so enraged she ordered all seven of the gates to be locked against her. To get through each gate Inanna had to remove one piece of her royal clothing. She eventually arrived at her sister's court humiliated, naked and powerless. Ereshkigal then killed Inanna and hung her body on a hook for all to see.

But, before visiting her sister, Inanna had made a cunning plan for her escape. She told a loyal servant to seek help from her father, who then sent his own servants to save her. It wasn't going to be easy. Ereshkigal demanded that Inanna find another person to take her place in the Underworld. When she returned to the land of the living, Inanna discovered the whole world believed she was dead. Everyone was upset, apart from one man – her own husband, Dumuzi, god of shepherds. Instead of mourning her, she discovered him sat on a grand throne in the finest clothes. In another fit of rage, Inanna threw him into the Underworld, transforming him into a snake, meaning she was free to return as Queen of Heaven.

SHAPING BELIEF

We know about Inanna from the myths that survive in clay tablets – some of the earliest writing ever discovered. She is goddess of rain, storms and the planet Venus, and is usually shown as a young beautiful woman, often riding a lion into battle. She's an independent, powerful, opinionated, strong-willed woman who does what she likes and is full of contradictions: sometimes kind, but sometimes vengeful, cruel and selfish.

An inscribed clay tablet, Iraq, 883–859 BC

ATHENA

Goddess of Wisdom and Guardian of Greece

A BIZARRE BIRTH

Athena is the Greek goddess of wisdom, warfare and weaving. She was also the protector of the ancient city named in her honour, Athens. She's usually shown fully armed and carrying weapons, with her sacred symbols – the wise owl and the sharp-eyed snake.

Her father, Zeus, was king of the gods. But Athena's mother, Metis, was also powerful and cunning and was once described as 'wiser than all gods and mortal men'. Zeus had heard a worrying rumour that any children he had with his first wife Metis would be incredibly wise, but they would also challenge his great power.

To get rid of this danger, he simply swallowed his pregnant wife. Zeus thought no more of Metis until some time later he began to feel the most terrible headaches.

Unable to suffer the pain any longer, he ordered Hephaestus, the god of blacksmiths, to crack open his head with an axe. Out sprang Athena from Zeus's skull – fully grown, dressed in armour and ready for battle.

WARRIOR WOMAN

Athena loved helping heroes and in one of the most famous stories of all, she helped Hercules in his 12 labours. Hercules was Athena's half-brother who had been driven mad by Zeus's wife, Hera. One day, feeling very confused and angry, Hercules killed his wife and children. Afterwards, he was wracked with guilt and begged forgiveness from the wise oracle of Delphi. As punishment, she told him to serve King Eurystheus for 12 years and complete the challenging tasks he set.

The labours were so difficult they seemed almost impossible. Hercules had to slay fearsome beasts, like the Nemean Lion and the Cretan Bull. But, bravely, he kept going and Athena helped out whenever she could. When Hercules was told to defeat a monstrous flock of man-eating birds, Athena gave him a sacred rattle. The loud noise scared the birds into the air so the hero could shoot them down with his arrows. Then he had to capture the fearsome three-headed dog Cerberus that guarded the Underworld. Again Athena came to the rescue. She gave Hercules some sweet honey cakes and when he fed them to the dog it fell straight to sleep and could be caught more easily.

In another story, fearless Athena went up against the sea god Poseidon in a competition. Each god had to give the city of Athens the best gift they could and King Cecrops would choose the winner. Poseidon struck his trident into the ground and water sprang up, giving the Athenians access to the sea and trade. But it was too salty to drink. Athena's gift was the very first olive tree in Greece. It provided wood, oil and food. King Cecrops decided that this was the better gift and Athena was declared the guardian goddess. She is sometimes shown with an olive tree, her precious gift to the Greek people and a symbol of peace.

A wine jug with Athena painted on its body, Greece, 470–460 BC

SHAPING BELIEF

The temple built to honour Athena on the hilltop Acropolis in Athens is a reminder of her influence. The Parthenon sculptures from there are some of the most well-known treasures of the ancient world and they are thought to show how the goddess was worshipped long ago. Originally, an enormous statue made from gold and ivory stood inside the temple and the priestesses who looked after it were some of the most important people in the city.

Every year, the Athenians honoured their courageous goddess with games and processions. The sacred statue would be dressed in a new gown, called a peplos, which the people of the city would spend months weaving with devotion. Today Athena remains an inspiring goddess. She represents calm wisdom, but she was also a ruthless warrior. She could be a very powerful enemy, but an even braver and more resourceful friend.

MAMI WATA

African Water Spirit and Bringer of Riches

SHAPE-SHIFTER

Mami Wata is a water spirit, whose West African roots may go back many hundreds, or even thousands, of years. She is now worshipped throughout Africa and African communities around the world. Over the last few centuries, her stories have been combined with European legends of mermaids as, like them, she is most at home in the sea.

So what does Mami Wata look like? Well, in fact, she has no single appearance and looks different to everyone who sees her. She is a spiritual force that belongs to the water, often shown as part human and part fish, but she can magically change her shape too – sometimes she appears fully human and sometimes she transforms into a man.

As a woman, she is dazzlingly beautiful, with large brilliant eyes and long flowing hair. Her beauty attracts both men and women and what she wants above all is complete devotion. Once you follow her, you may be trapped forever.

One story tells how Mami Wata catches people at sea and takes them to a paradise, either underwater or in the spirit realm. Here she insists they stay faithful and worship no others. If she allows them to return to the human world, they must continue to honour Mami Wata – and only Mami Wata. Then they will become more attractive, richer and healthier than ever before. But if they dare to betray her, they will soon fall ill and die. Her moods can change quickly – from generous, creative and kind to cruel and jealous.

MIRRORS AND MOTIFS

Mami Wata transforms to the needs of those around her. She brings different things to different people and her stories are as varied as those that honour her. If you want a child, she can help. If you want gold, turn to her. If you want to be adored, she is there for those that honour her.

A wooden carving of Mami Wata

Her most important symbol is the mirror. Through a mirror's shiny surface, the water spirits and those that worship them can connect directly and journey between realms and through time. Mirrors are a meeting point between water and land, past and future, the world above the ocean and Mami Wata's world below it.

Mami Wata is often shown with a huge python wrapped round her. The snake is a symbol of her power and connection to nature. As a water spirit who moves up rivers and through the sea, she is a source of life. Her waters also connect people as Mami Wata controls the highways of riches, bringing trade, travel, goods and wealth. But, like the ocean, she can be unpredictable. What she gives she can also take away in an instant.

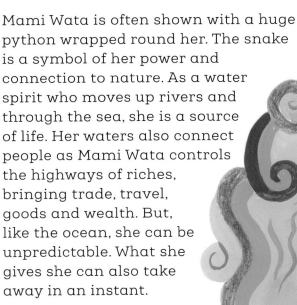

SHAPING BELIEF

People honour Mami Wata by giving her expensive gifts or offerings, and holding ceremonies with intense music, guitar playing and dancing that can send people into a trance. This dream-like state allows followers to communicate with Mami Wata and ask for her protection. Out of respect, some communities in Africa avoid fishing or going to the beach on certain days as they believe this gives some peace to the water spirit's home.

When people were forcibly enslaved as part of the transatlantic slave trade, Mami Wata protected them. She is now worshipped throughout the Americas in different ways, such as the Yemanja festival in Brazil that celebrates the sea and Mami Wata as a water spirit. She is a powerful woman, bringing help to those who need it and rewarding those who give her their devotion.

NUT

Ancient Egyptian Goddess of the Sky

BORN OF AIR AND MOISTURE

Nut is one of the oldest goddesses in ancient Egypt. She is a member of the Ennead, a group of nine gods and goddesses of the ancient city of Heliopolis, near to Cairo. Her parents were created by the first god, Atum. Her father was Shu, god of dry air, and her mother was Tefnut, goddess of moisture. Together they formed the sky above, Nut, and the ground below, her brother Geb.

She is made of the elements and stars, and the universe covers her body. She arches over the earth, touching it just with the very tips of her fingers and toes. In most religions the sky is a male god while the earth is female, so Nut's femininity is incredibly unusual. She passes the sun through her body every day and night, giving birth to it as mother of the heavenly bodies. In fact, it's her role as mother that made Nut so essential to the ancient Egyptians.

MOTHER OF GODS

The sun god, Ra, feared anyone taking his power. When he heard Nut was going to have children, he was afraid they would challenge him, so he cursed her, saying, "Nut shall not give birth any day of the year." The Egyptian year at that point was 360 days long. How could she possibly have her children if she could not give birth on any day? She came up with a plan, conspiring with the clever bird-headed god of wisdom, Thoth. He was in love with Nut so did not hesitate to help. Thoth promised to beat the god of the moon, Khonsu, at gambling. Whenever he lost, Khonsu had to give Thoth part of his moonlight. Khonsu was not very good at rolling dice and lost time and time again. Soon enough Thoth had won enough moonlight for five extra days.

In each of these five days Nut gave birth to one of her children, and a new generation of powerful gods and goddesses were born. Ra was so furious at being deceived that he promised to forever separate Nut from her brother and husband, Geb. He made their father, Shu, god of dry air, lie between them so earth and sky could never be reunited. While Nut and Geb pine for each other day and night, they can never be together.

As a loving mother, Nut tried to help her children whenever she could. However, the children turned on one another. One of her sons, Seth, killed her most beloved child Osiris. After her daughter Isis lovingly put him back together, Osiris climbed a ladder (a sacred symbol of Nut) to enter her heavenly skies for protection. Because of this Nut became known as protector of the dead.

SHAPING BELIEF

Nut is also known as 'one with a thousand souls', since the souls of the dead were represented as stars in the sky. She is 'Mother of the Gods' and the ceiling of ancient Egyptian graves and coffins often show an image of her stretching over the dead body like the heavens.

Nut doesn't only give birth and watch over death, though. She also provides nutrition for her children so they grow through life. This means she is sometimes shown as a great cow stretching across the sky or a sow suckling her piglets, who are the stars. She is also the sycamore tree, providing shelter to those who need it.

A coffin with Nut painted below the collar, Egypt, 600 BC

Her connection to the heavens was scientific too, and the ancient Egyptians called their study of time, the planets and the stars the 'Book of Nut'. The goddess still inspires women today, who celebrate her as the mother of the stars, moon and sun.

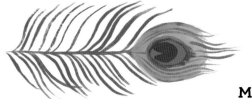

JUNO

Mother Goddess of Rome and Protector of Women

GUARDIAN OF ROME

As the protective goddess of the city of Rome, Juno is a complex figure whose myths, stories and character change depending on where across the huge Roman Empire she was honoured.

The equivalent of Hera in Greek mythology, Juno was married to the chief of the gods – Jupiter. He was her brother and, with their siblings, Neptune, Pluto, Vesta and Ceres, she was a daughter of the sky god, Saturn. Alongside her husband and the goddess of wisdom, Minerva, Juno was one of the Capitoline Triad, worshipped in an elaborate temple on one of Rome's famous seven hills.

Juno's name is most probably connected to the idea of youth, although she is also goddess of love and marriage. Sometimes called 'queen', she appears on Roman coins as the image of the perfect female ruler. As mother of Rome, she looked after all the people of the state, but she was particularly honoured by women. She protected them from the cradle to the grave, helping women through childbirth and blessing their marriages.

MORE THAN A MOTHER

Alongside Mars, god of war, and Vulcan, god of fire, Juno and Jupiter were the most important of Rome's gods and goddesses. Jupiter was not always a faithful husband, though. It's even said that he created fog so Juno couldn't see him being unfaithful to her with other women. Rightfully angry at her husband's cheating ways, fiercely loyal Juno tried to catch him out many times.

A bronze bust of Juno, Italy, 300–100 BC

In one story, Jupiter had fallen for a priestess called Io. To protect Io from his wife's jealousy, Jupiter transformed Io into a cow, but Juno uncovered his plan. She wanted to keep a constant eye on her husband's lover, so she sent a giant with 100 eyes called Argus to watch over him.

When Jupiter found out what his wife had been plotting, he sent his messenger, Mercury, to kill the monster. Juno was so distraught at the murder of her faithful watchman that she took each of his 100 eyes and put them in the tail of a peacock. This became a symbol of the goddess, as a reminder of her most loyal servant.

In Virgil's famous epic tale, *The Aeneid*, Juno went out of her way to frustrate attempts by the hero, Aeneas, to found the city of Rome in Italy. She lured Aeneas to Carthage, where he fell head over heels in love with the beautiful queen Dido. Yet, even though he'd met Dido, Aeneas was still determined to fulfil his prophecy in Rome, so he tore himself away and left for Italy. Overcome with grief, Dido built a funeral pyre and, on top of it, took Aeneas's sword and plunged it through her body. Juno's interfering led to Dido's death and shows how she could sometimes be cruel.

SHAPING BELIEF

In ancient Rome, Juno's main festival was celebrated on the first of March. It was called the Matronalia. Women were allowed to wear their hair loose and received gifts from their husbands and children – it was like a Roman version of Mother's Day.

Juno also had other festivals on the first of the month throughout the year which were connected with the waxing and waning of the moon. This is because people believed Juno controlled the cycles of the months and the coming of the seasons.

Like all Roman gods and goddesses, Juno had many different sides to her character. She's best known for being kind and motherly as the goddess of childbirth and marriage, yet she could also be cruel and jealous – a goddess as changeable as the moon.

EZILI DANTÒ

Haiti's Vodou Goddess of Vengeance and Motherhood

BLENDING CULTURES

In Haitian Vodou, Ezili Dantò is a spirit, or *lwa*. She represents the beauty and the trials of motherhood and brings comfort and strength to single mothers in particular. She has a wide range of emotions and can sometimes be filled with a vengeful rage.

To understand Ezili Dantò, you first need to understand Vodou (or Vodún), which means 'spirit' or 'sacred energy' in the Fon language of Benin. During the 1500s–1800s, when enslaved African people took their religions with them to Saint-Domingue (now Haiti), Vodou was born from a combination of Fon, Yoruba and Kongo traditions of West and Central Africa, as well as the Taino traditions of the Caribbean. The French people that colonised the island of Haiti were Catholic, so Africans were forced to combine African gods and goddesses with Catholic saints in Vodou.

Some Vodou spirits have ancient roots, while others, like Ezili Dantò, represent the more recent set of spirits, born out of slavery, rebellion and revolution. These spirits understand the harsh conditions that enslaved African people had to endure under French colonisation.

THE FREEDOM FIGHTER

To honour the spirits and ancestors, priests, priestesses and devotees take part in ceremonies. Here they are visited by spirits that deliver messages through a ritual called 'mounting'. Connecting with Ezili Dantò in this way can produce powerful results, such as the Haitian Revolution – the only successful slave revolt in the world, which led to Haiti's independence from France.

Ezili Dantò played an important part in bringing freedom to her people when enslaved Haitians came together to overthrow their oppressors. They made offerings to the spirits in a ceremony where Ezili Dantò sent a message to the priestess, and everyone agreed to fight for their freedom. Some people say that Ezili Dantò joined the fighting herself, disguised as a man, and when soldiers discovered her identity, they cut out her tongue for fear she would reveal their secrets. This left the goddess with two scars on her cheek and unable to speak – she could only make a clicking noise with her mouth. Haiti finally gained its independence in 1804, after 13 years of war, with help from Ezili Dantò, the freedom fighter.

Many pictures of Ezili Dantò show her as the Black Madonna of Czestochowa, the patron saint of Poland. This is because, as Haitian soldiers fought for their independence, Polish soldiers who had been recruited by the French leader Napoleon broke ties with the French army and joined Haitian forces. They had brought prints of the Black Madonna with them and in them Vodou devotees saw the image of Ezili Dantò – a loving mother with her child in her arms.

SHAPING BELIEF

Ezili Dantò has two children – a daughter called Anais and a son called Ti Jean Petwo. Because Ezili Dantò can't speak, Anais speaks for her and is usually shown alongside her. Ezili Dantò's sister is Ezili Freda, the goddess of love, beauty and riches. The sisters are opposite in many ways – Freda is graceful, pleasure-loving and luxurious, whereas Ezili Dantò is strongly built, hard-working and resilient.

As one of the most powerful and important Vodou spirits, Ezili Dantò's image has been blended with the most important of Christian women: the Virgin Mary. Often she is represented by a heart pierced with a dagger, while her sister Ezili Freda is shown as a heart of love.

A fearless warrior and freedom fighter, Ezili Dantò is above all a loving mother who will do anything for her children. She provides them with the courage and strength to conquer whatever stands in their path.

A Haitian 10 gourdes bill showing Suzanne "Sanité" Bélair, a revolutionary female freedom fighter, Haiti

RHIANNON

Welsh Queen of Horses and Courage

OUT OF REACH

Rhiannon is a fascinating character from the famous medieval Welsh poem *The Mabinogion*. This collection of fantastical stories deals with everything from ancient history to romance, but woven into the tales are religious ideas much older than the poem, which go back thousands of years to Wales's Celtic past.

A goddess of the Otherworld – a place just like the real world but with strange variations – Rhiannon is a particularly self-confident and empowered woman.

In the poem, she first appears on a sacred hill, riding a magnificent white horse and dressed in golden silk. The Lord of Dyfed, Pwyll, tells his riders to capture the beautiful woman. For days they chase her, but although Rhiannon's horse never went faster than a walk, the men could not catch up.

Finally Pwyll himself cried out to Rhiannon to stop. She halted her horse and said mockingly that he should have done that from the start. She had come for Pwyll alone because she wanted him as her husband. But there's a twist in the tale! Rhiannon was already promised to marry another man – Gwawl. How could she stop this wedding from going ahead?

She organised a special wedding feast and told Pwyll to dress as a beggar. When he arrived at the celebration, Pwyll asked Gwawl to fill a small bag with food. Gwawl tried to help the hungry man, but the bag was enchanted. He simply couldn't fill it. Eventually Gwawl stepped inside the bag himself, to see what magic controlled it. Of course, Pwyll seized the moment and called his soldiers from outside.

They played the medieval game of 'badger in the bag' – kicking and beating the sack with Gwawl inside, until he crawled out covered in cuts and bruises. Gwawl soon realised that marrying Rhiannon was probably not the wisest idea after all, so instead Rhiannon got what she wanted and became queen of Dyfed.

WRONGFULLY ACCUSED

Three years later, Rhiannon gave birth to a baby boy. On the first night, while she slept, her newborn son mysteriously disappeared from his cradle. The maids had fallen asleep too. Afraid they would be blamed, they killed a puppy and smeared its blood on Rhiannon to make it look like she had eaten her own son. Devastated by the loss of her only child, Rhiannon agreed to be punished. Every day, she sat by the stables and told her story to passers-by. She even carried visitors on her back, like a horse, which was humiliating for a queen. But through it all Pwyll continued to love and honour her.

And then, in another twist, Rhiannon's son was found. He had been fostered by another Welsh lord. As the baby grew, he started to look exactly like his true father, so he was returned to his rightful parents and named Pryderi, after the first words Rhiannon uttered on seeing him, "now all my worries are gone".

SHAPING BELIEF

Rhiannon has a very strong bond with horses. In fact, she can even enchant them. She and Pryderi are often shown as a mother horse with her foal, so some people think that she might be a later Welsh version of the Celtic horse goddess Epona. Both goddesses are referred to as 'queen' and are often seen sitting on a horse that is moving carefully and gracefully.

Epona was worshipped across Celtic Europe and it's possible that her legacy lived on in the medieval tales of Rhiannon. For many Welsh people Rhiannon is a strong and complex woman whose stories still inspire pride and fascination.

XIWANGMU

China's Tao Goddess of Life, Death, Creation and Destruction

THE PALACE IN THE MOUNTAINS

There are few more important goddesses in China than Xiwangmu, queen mother of the West. First mentioned in inscriptions over 3,000 years old, she is described as a fierce character with tiger teeth and a leopard's tail who could bring plague and disease to those who displeased her. But over time she transformed into a gentler figure connected to paradise and eternal life.

Taoism is an ancient Chinese tradition of philosophy and religious beliefs that emphasises living in harmony with nature. Existence is made up of essential opposites: light and dark, hot and cold, wet and dry. These things depend on each other and don't make sense on their own. This is the principle of yin and yang. The goddess Xiwangmu is yin. She is the feminine and the air from the west. The heavenly yang is her husband, the Jade Emperor and ruler of heaven. Together they determine everything, including birth, death and immortality.

Xiwangmu is known by different names, including Golden Mother. She is stunningly beautiful and her home is in the mythical Kunlun Mountains, where her palace is full of love, laughter and life.

In her happy court, the goddess is surrounded by wondrous things. Phoenixes spread their fiery feathers – they constantly burst into flames and are perfectly reborn. Her ladies-in-waiting dance around the Turquoise Pond while magical beasts explore the forests. There are nine floors to her palace, which is made of the precious green stone jade. It's surrounded by fairyland gardens, with a lake bursting with lotus flowers.

FRUIT OF ETERNAL LIFE

An ivory figure of Xiwangmu, China, 1662–1722

Xiwangmu has a very important job. She has to look after the trees in her garden that grow the Peaches of Immortality. These fruits are so rare they only appear once every 3,000 years. Each year at her birthday feast she feeds peaches to the gods so they can continue to live. Without her and the fruits that she harvests, the gods would eventually become mortal and die.

But it isn't just the gods that Xiwangmu looks after. Her peach tree is also the only place where humans and gods can communicate. Here she offers advice, guidance and protection to Chinese emperors, teaching them the secrets of eternal life. No matter what wisdom and learning she gives them, the emperors always fail her tests and remain mortal.

Xiwangmu did give the emperors the 'Mandate of Heaven', though, which meant they had support from heaven to rule on earth. Many thousands of years ago, the emperor Shun said that Xiwangmu had given him the mandate herself. When he was crowned, she aligned five planets in the sky as a sign of her support. Claiming they had the love of such a powerful goddess was a great way for an emperor to hold on to power.

SHAPING BELIEF

Xiwangmu is a creator goddess. She has a talent for weaving and people believe that every night she weaves the stars into the sky. She wears her loom as a headdress, and if it were ever to break, all the fabric of creation that Xiwangmu has lovingly crafted would fall apart. But she is even more important for her role in spreading wisdom, achieving immortality and protecting humans on earth, especially rulers.

To many people in China, Xiwangmu is an inspiring figure, because she shows how much power one woman can have. If couples pray to her, she can send them a child. But she is never happy if they ask for a male baby instead of a female one; she sees girls and boys as equally important – yin and yang.

BABA YAGA

Villain and Protector, the Wicked Witch of Russian Folklore

TERRIFYING TO BEHOLD

If you've read any folk tales from Russia and Eastern Europe, you will probably have heard of the famous witch Baba Yaga. She features in many stories, sometimes as an old woman, sometimes as three identical women or sometimes even as sisters. The mysterious, magical Baba Yaga is a powerful woman who isn't loyal to anyone. While some people visit her for advice, she is dangerous so they have to tread carefully – she may decide to help you but, more often, she will try to eat you.

One of the strangest things about Baba Yaga is where she lives. Her hut lies deep in a forest, turns around like a spinning top and has chicken legs sticking out of the bottom! The legs mean that the house can run away and hide. Anyone going to visit her must have a great need if they are prepared to enter such a strange building.

But that's not the only thing that might sound like a nightmare ... Baba Yaga looks terrifying too. She has long arms and legs that spread from one side of her hut to the other, with a pointed nose that touches the ceiling so she can sniff whoever is brave enough to visit. Sometimes she flies through the air inside a bowl used for grinding herbs, a mortar, with the grinding stick – the pestle – to steer her.

TWINS IN TROUBLE

In one famous story, a pair of young twins were sent into the deep, dark forest to find Baba Yaga's hut. Their father had married a woman who wanted to get rid of them once and for all. Before the twins set out, their beloved grandmother gave them some advice: "Be kind and good to everyone; do not speak bad words to anyone; help the weakest, and always hope that you too will get help."

Alone and afraid, the children walked through the wood... until eventually they reached the hut with the chicken legs. There was a fence made of skulls around the outside and soon the terrifying Baba Yaga came out to greet them. She said she would gobble them up unless they did the chores she set.

The girl was set to work weaving yarn, and the boy had to fill a bath with water using a sieve with holes in it. Every time he tried, the water simply trickled away and he was scared he would be eaten.

"Give us some crumbs and we will help you," some friendly birds chirped as they flew by. The boy quickly handed over a few crumbs and, in exchange, the birds told him to put some clay inside the sieve. Soon the boy was able to fill up the whole bathtub.

When Baba Yaga saw how hard the children had worked, she agreed she would not eat them as she had to keep her promise. Instead she said she would set even harder tasks the next day. But the animals of the forest remembered the children's kindness and helped the twins escape.

SHAPING BELIEF

Terrifying and unpredictable, Baba Yaga has haunted children and adults for centuries. In most stories, people only visit her spinning hut when they need something. The greater their wish, the harder their tasks, but often their kindness and hard work help them to survive. Whether a witch or goddess, Baba Yaga remains one of the most mysterious characters in Russian folklore.

A stamp showing Baba Yaga, illustrated by Ivan Bilibin, Russia, about 1984

DURGA

Hindu Goddess of Supreme Power, Protection and Strength

INVINCIBLE WARRIOR

Some Hindu texts written over 1,000 years ago say that creation didn't begin with a male god but with a female goddess. In the branch of Hinduism known as Shaktism, the source of spiritual energy is female. This power takes many forms, and one of the most important is the goddess Durga. She's the unbeatable slayer of demons. With her ultimate blend of peace and war, she is both loving mother and warrior goddess who protects those in need.

The name Durga means 'impassable' or 'invincible'. The most famous story about her tells how she managed to kill the demon buffalo Mahishasura. It begins when a cruel king of the Underworld and a beautiful princess, who was cursed to take the form of a buffalo, had a son – Mahishasura. He could transform from man to buffalo whenever he wanted.

Mahishasura hated the gods and decided to become the most powerful of demons so he could destroy them. First he needed to gain their trust, so he offered penance to the high god – Brahma. He chanted, prayed and meditated for many years and Brahma could not ignore his devotion. As a reward for his efforts. Brahma offered Mahishasura any wish he desired. "Make it so no man or god can ever defeat me," Mahishasura replied. Brahma agreed and the demon buffalo gained supernatural powers that made him undefeatable.

DEFEATER OF DEMONS

Mahishasura spread chaos across the world. No one could stop him as he transformed from man to buffalo, charging up to the homes of the gods. They sat in terror, realising that Brahma's promise could not be broken. Then they thought very carefully about exactly what had been promised – no man or god could destroy Mahishasura, but a woman or a goddess could! Each god sent out a ray of light and as they met with a crash of thunder Durga appeared.

She was the power of creation, preservation and destruction. Durga was devastatingly beautiful. She had long dark hair and was covered in precious jewellery and garlands of marigolds. To help her, each god gave her a gift. While some, like the sword, spear and club, were weapons designed to bring victory in battle, others, like the conch shell, bell and lotus flower, show her importance for discovering inner peace.

A bronze figure of Durga, India, 1100–1300

The Lord of the Himalayas, her father Himavant, gave her a fierce lion. Durga leaped on its back, grabbed her precious gifts in her many hands and blew her conch shell with a deafening sound. Striding towards the demon buffalo's army, her feet left craters in the ground.

The heavens shook as she filled the earth and sky with her radiant light.
She called an army of warriors to help and together they destroyed Mahishasura's
troops. But there was still the demon buffalo – and Durga was the only one powerful enough to take
him on. After a fierce fight, she was able to cut off Mahishasura's head, defeating evil, destruction
and cruelty. She remained calm and tranquil because her violence was not driven by hatred, but by
love for the world she was protecting.

SHAPING BELIEF

In Bengal, India, the Durga Puja is
a Hindu festival that takes place
in autumn and lasts for 10 days.
It's dedicated to the goddess and
magnificent, temporary images of
her are made out of clay. They are
displayed in shrines and then placed
in rivers at the end of the festival to
ensure a good harvest. The festival
celebrates Durga's victory over evil,
but also her role as creator. People
pray that the goddess,
both motherly and
victorious, will provide
for the coming year and
return next year.

With her independence
and strength as a warrior,
Durga challenges
the role of women as
gentle, caring mothers,
wives or daughters.
Yet she has all these
qualities too, so is the
ultimate role model for
women who want to be
strong and kind, loving
and unstoppable.

VENUS
Roman Goddess of Love, Beauty and Victory

MOTHER OF ROME

You might have heard about the goddess Venus before. Centuries of artists and sculptors have shown her naked – the perfect female. But Venus isn't simply a beautiful woman for others to gaze at. She is a powerful, unpredictable and important goddess. The Romans took many of the myths connected to the mysterious Greek goddess of love, Aphrodite, and added flourishes of their own to create Venus – a goddess of earthly love and heavenly devotion.

At the very heart of the ancient Roman religion Venus's myths tell how she had many lovers, both humans and gods, and gave birth to the child god Cupid. She also helped heroes like her son Aeneas, guiding him on his journey from Troy to Rome. Aeneas was an ancestor of Romulus and Remus, the founders of Rome, so Venus is known as 'bringer of victory' and 'Mother of Rome'.

Venus's birth isn't like any other god or goddess. She was 'born from foam'. One story tells how Terra, mother of all life on earth, was furious at her husband Caelus. He kept their children prisoners because he didn't want any of them to overthrow him. But one day Terra handed one of her sons a sharp knife, telling him to cut up Caelus's body and throw the parts in the sea. When the water mixed with Caelus's flesh, it created a foam and out of it emerged Venus, fully formed and beautiful. As she walked on to the shores of Cyprus, flowers sprung up wherever her feet touched the ground.

THE GOLDEN APPLE

In a famous story, Venus plays a part in one of the most important mythological events – the great Trojan War. Jupiter was throwing a big wedding feast but didn't invite Discordia, goddess of strife, as he knew she would ruin the party. But Discordia heard the celebrations and, determined to get her revenge, turned up with a golden apple she had taken from the garden of the nymphs. She announced a beauty contest – whoever was declared the most beautiful would win the golden apple.

Three goddesses came forward – Juno (Jupiter's wife), Minerva (goddess of wisdom) and Venus. Jupiter said he simply couldn't judge, so asked a Trojan prince named Paris to make the decision. Each of the goddesses tried to bribe Paris. Juno offered him the crown of Europe and Asia. Minerva offered him wisdom and victory in war. But Venus offered him the love of the most beautiful woman in the world: Helen, the wife of a Greek king. This was a hard choice. Paris could have worldly power or great wisdom. Instead he dangerously chose love. Paris declared Venus winner of the contest. He then went to claim his beautiful wife, kidnapping her, and so began the long and bloody war between Greece and Troy. This story shows that the gift of Venus's love can be both a blessing and a curse.

SHAPING BELIEF

The Romans saw Venus as a goddess who could guide them to greatness and help them in battle. As one of the most important Roman goddesess, she was honoured across the empire. Emperors also realised that it would be helpful to have Venus on their side. The first emperor, Julius Caesar, tied his family to her son Aeneas, showing that he was descended from Venus herself. He built temples in her honour and even had her face stamped on his coins. In this way, Venus was so much more than a goddess of love – she was a powerful ancestor who protected the Roman Empire.

Festivals to celebrate Venus took place in April and she welcomed in the springtime. Many of her ceremonies involved drinking wine and offering up gifts of fruit and vegetables. Young girls would hang garlands round statues of the goddess. To this day, she is celebrated as a powerful woman, who balances the fires of passion, war and violence with love, gentleness and kindness.

A marble statue of Venus de Milo by Alexandros of Antioch, Greece, 130 BC

29

CHALCHIUHTLIQUE

Aztec Goddess of Fresh Water

A stone figure of Chalchiuhtlique, Mexico, 1325–1521

PROVIDER AND DESTROYER

Chalchiuhtlique was an important water goddess for the Aztecs of ancient Mexico. In the many sculptures of her that survive, she's often shown wearing a green skirt. In fact, her name means 'she who wears the jade skirt'. In ancient Mexico, jade was more precious than gold, and its green colour represented water. Chalchiuhtlique protected rivers, lakes and safe travels across the seas, but water also carried many sacred meanings. It could wash away sins and it played a part in the cycle of life and death, which is why Chalchiuhtlique was also said to look after mothers and their newborn babies.

The water goddess is linked to the powerful, temperamental and unpredictable god of rain and lightning, Tlaloc. In some myths, she is his wife, in some she is his sister, and in others they are two parts of the same deity, or god. As a team they control four types of water: the first was life-giving, the second drowned plants, the third brought frost and the fourth could destroy everything.

Like the water she represents, Chalchiuhtlique could make both positive and negative things happen. She lived at the very top of a mountain and when she released her precious water to the fields below it brought new life, but she could also destroy the land by sending storms and rain. When she was paired with the corn goddess Xilonen, she brought the harvest, but when she was paired with the dangerous snake goddess Chicomecoatl, she could bring disastrous drought. She's also known for creating whirlpools and violent storms, making it hard for sailors to cross the seas.

A DEVASTATING FLOOD

Chalchiuhtlique's most famous story is connected with a flood that transformed all the people into marvellous new species of fish. It starts by saying that humans live in an age known as the Fifth Sun. Before this, the early gods and goddesses had made four different versions of the world, but destroyed each one by battling between themselves. Chalchiuhtlique ruled over the Fourth Sun, or Fourth Age. This world was devastated by a great flood when Chalchiuhtlique poured down a rain so powerful humans became fish and the sky and heavens fell and had to be propped back up again by other gods.

Chalchiuhtlique and her husband Tlaloc lived in the paradise called Tlalocan and here they welcomed anyone who had died a watery death. People who travelled to Tlalocan were not cremated, or burned, like most people were at this time in Mesoamerica. Instead their drowned bodies were buried whole and dressed in paper, with seeds planted on their faces and blue paint on their foreheads. In the afterlife, at Chalchiuhtlique's water paradise, they would receive only the very best, taking their pick of the feast for all eternity.

SHAPING BELIEF

The sixth month of the Aztec calendar, when the rainy season begins in Mexico, was dedicated to Chalchiuhtlique.

People hoped to please the goddess and encouraged the fields to ripen through prayers and offerings. Celebrations and feasts were held around lagoons, with special objects placed into the water as gifts.

But there was also a terrifying aspect to her ceremonies. During one – Atlcahualo – many children were taken to sacred mountaintops and killed. If these children cried on the way to the shrine, their tears were seen as a positive sign that the life-giving rains would come soon.

Chalchiuhtlique was one of the most popular Aztec goddesses when the Spanish arrived and eventually colonised the Aztec Empire in 1521. Images of Chalchiuhtlique show her with a large tasselled headdress and a blue-green flowing skirt. Sometimes, in paintings, newborn babies are shown floating in the water alongside Chalchiuhtlique. This could be because young children were offered to the goddess as a gift during ceremonies, or it could be because of the powerful protection she gave women and their babies.

BRIGID

Celtic Goddess of the Elements, Healing and Poetry

FIRE, EARTH AND WATER

In the UK and Ireland, Brigid is one of the most popular goddesses whose tales have been told for thousands of years. Her father was the mysterious god of magic and wisdom, the Dagda, while her mother was a poet who gave her the gift of weaving words. Brigid was the goddess of spring, the dawn, medicine, poetry and the natural elements – earth, water and fire. Known as the 'High One' or the 'Goddess of the Well', she's connected with hills and mountains, rivers and waterways. But, flame-haired and wearing a cloak of bright sunbeams, Brigid is best known for being worshipped with fire.

In some legends Brigid was married to the High King Bres, and together they had a son named Ruadán. Shortly after arriving in Ireland, the gods began to battle with a tribe of fearsome, hideous monsters and Brigid's son was killed. She ran on to the battlefield shrieking and weeping and her loud cries became known as 'keening' – a wailing song of grief that inspired many poets and musicians through the ages and could often be heard at funerals.

Brigid's role as an earth mother was very important. She was honoured for her wisdom in many areas, inspiring artists, architects, metalworkers and craftspeople of all trades. If you had a pure heart and a busy mind, Brigid would be the goddess that helped you. She protected the people, the land and animals. In fact, she was the guardian goddess of pets and had her own special animals to look after – two oxen named Fe and Men; a pig named Torc Triath, 'king of the boars'; and a powerful ram, Cirb, ruler of all sheep.

FROM GODDESS TO SAINT

Many people believe there is a connection between the goddess and a later Christian saint of the same name, Brigid of Kildare. Saint Brigid is very important as one of the patron saints of Ireland and records of her life say she had miraculous powers.

She could hang her cloak on a sunbeam and the nuns at her abbey kept an eternal flame burning for her, guarding it day and night. Her sanctuary was ringed with a circle of bushes and no man was allowed inside or they would burst into flames. So the goddess and saint share a connection with fire.

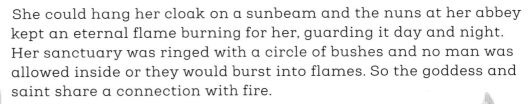

But the most unusual thing about Saint Brigid was that she had similar powers to a bishop, a very important member of the Christian church. This was rare for women at the time, so Saint Brigid, like the goddess who came before her, continued to be a symbol of female power. While many pagan practices were wiped out when Ireland converted to Christianity, the importance of Brigid lived on.

SHAPING BELIEF

Each year on the first of February there is a special feast day for both saint and goddess Brigid, known as 'Imbolc'. It marks the beginning of spring. Candles and fires are lit to represent the sun getting hotter, and people visit sacred wells to leave gifts and bless themselves with holy water. Nowadays, to honour the saint, people weave crosses out of grass and buy dolls stuffed with hay, which are carried from house-to-house to ward off evil. Brigid was a much-loved goddess who gave her name to a saint because she was too important to ever be forgotten.

A cross of Saint Brigid woven from rushes, Ireland

PATTINI

Sri Lankan Goddess of Purity and Fighter Against Injustice

LOYAL WIFE

Pattini's tale is full of tragedy and drama, but at its heart is a love story between an ordinary woman and her husband. Before she was worshipped as a goddess, Pattini was called Kannagi and her life was recorded in one of the oldest pieces of literature to survive from Sri Lanka – the *Cilappatikaram*, which means 'The Jewelled Anklet'. This beautiful epic poem tells how Kannagi married the son of a merchant, Kovalan, while they were very young.

They lived happily together until one day Kovalan caught a glimpse of a beautiful dancing woman named Madhavi. He fell madly in love with her at once. In his desire, he left his wife and began spending all their money on his new love. Kannagi was heartbroken, but she swore she would remain loyal and wait for her husband to return.

Soon fortune turned in her favour. Kovalan returned to his wife, embarrassed and begging for forgiveness. Though she was hurt, she realised that she wanted to stand by him, so they began planning their future together, but there was one big problem – now they had no money. Kannagi remembered she still had a pair of precious ankle bracelets made of solid gold and set with jewels. Desperate to get their lives back on track, she unfastened one of them and gave it to Kovalan so that he could sell it and buy what they needed to survive.

SEEKING REVENGE

This is where it all went wrong. When the people of the city saw Kannagi's anklet they said it was so beautiful and precious that it must be the queen's missing treasure. It must have been stolen! Kovalan was arrested as a thief and killed without any chance to defend himself. The news soon reached Kannagi who flew towards the city in a rage.

Grieving, furious and fierce, Kannagi stormed into the palace and bravely stood before the king. Here she took off her other jewelled anklet to show him. The queen's missing bracelet had pearls encrusted in it, while Kannagi's sparkled with rubies. It was all a mistake – her husband had died for nothing. As her sense of injustice grew, Kannagi became wild with passion. In front of everyone she called on Agni, the god of fire, to destroy the city. Seeing Kannagi's loyalty, endurance and nobility, the god heard her cry. Buildings instantly burst into flames and soon the whole city was a fiery inferno. Only the good people were saved while the wicked burned. Kannagi had received justice.

SHAPING BELIEF

But what happened next to Kannagi? Does her story have a happy ending? Well, she was taken to heaven where she became the goddess, Pattini – one of the most popular goddesses in Sri Lanka. Today people still honour her with many different rituals.

In some villages, people act out her story, and in others they play games with coconuts, sticks or horns. The games vary, but one side always plays as the goddess, while the other acts as the husband or the wicked king. Through these games the people of Sri Lanka continue to celebrate the bravery and faithfulness of Pattini.

Although Pattini suffered greatly, she remained strong and stood up for truth. She's often shown holding her two treasured anklets as a sign of her loyalty, and she provides hope and support to women who also find themselves fighting injustice.

A bracelet made from crystal and silver, Sri Lanka

ARIADNE

Cretan Goddess of Labyrinths and Mazes

SISTER OF A MONSTER

Ariadne is recorded in Greek myths, but her story may go back thousands of years to an earlier Minoan mother goddess from the island of Crete. In the older language of the island, *Ariadne* means 'most holy one'. In later legends she became a princess of the Mediterranean island and daughter of its legendary king, Minos.

Minos was a son of Zeus, chief of the gods, when he had transformed into a bull. In fact, bulls feature in many of the stories about Ariadne.

Minos's wife and Ariadne's mother, Pasiphae, fell in love with another bull and later gave birth to her half-brother, the minotaur – half man, half bull. Terrified of this dangerous creature, Minos built a huge labyrinth underneath his palace to keep it prisoner. The minotaur was fed with the flesh of young men and women, and the people of Crete lived in fear that it could one day escape to terrorise the island. Ariadne, the monster's half-sister, was put in charge of the minotaur's maze.

An amphora painted with Ariadne, Theseus and the Minotaur, Greece, 510–500 BC

IN LOVE WITH A HERO

In one story, a Greek hero called Theseus decided he would destroy the minotaur once and for all. When sacrifices were called for from Athens, he went willingly, knowing he would be given to the minotaur as food. As soon as she saw the heroic Theseus, Ariadne immediately fell in love with him and vowed to help in his mission to kill the beast. She gave him a ball of wool, made by Hephaestus, the god of blacksmiths. If he left a trail of wool as he walked and then followed it back again, he would be able to find his way out of the bewildering maze.

Ariadne also gave Theseus a sword, and with this sharp blade he was able to cut the bull's head from the minotaur's body.

Knowing she had betrayed her father and her country, Ariadne escaped from Crete with Theseus. But he was very unkind. He abandoned her in the middle of the sea, where she sat wailing sorrowfully on an island.

The god of wine, Dionysus, discovered Ariadne and, seeing her beauty, married her. Some stories say they were already destined to end up together, while others say Dionysus rescued Ariadne. The wedding tiara she wore became the beautiful constellation of stars known as the 'Corona Borealis'. They had many children together and Dionysus loved her so much that when she died he made her immortal. He placed her headdress in the sky so everyone would know about their eternal love.

SHAPING BELIEF

With the magical wool that she used to help Theseus, Ariadne became linked with the mystical art of weaving. Her name may also link to the similar sounding *arachne*, which means spider, as she spun the fate of all those around her.

When the remarkable palace of Knossos in Crete was discovered just over 100 years ago, archaeologists found figurines of mother goddesses much older than ancient Greek civilisation, which date back nearly 4,000 years. Clay tablets that still haven't been fully decoded include the name 'A-sa-sa-ra'. Is this the name of the long-lost goddess of Crete? And was she transformed into Ariadne over the centuries? What the female figurines and Ariadne's tales tell us is that on the island of Crete women were among the most important religious figures.

ASASE YAA

West African Goddess of the Earth

OUT OF REACH

Asase Yaa is the earth goddess of the Akan people in Ghana. She is also known as Aberewa (old woman) and is the wife of the sky god, Onyame. Queens ruled the first Akan kingdoms, until power was transferred to male rulers. The gods reflect the way power is ordered even now – Onyame is king and Asase Yaa is queen mother. She shares his power and he has no power over her. Authority passes through the mother's line, so traditionally women are given great respect and can still act as rulers.

Why can't we touch the sky from the earth? The Akan say it's because of a story that begins with Asase Yaa pounding food in a mortar, hammering it over and over with a stone pestle. As she moved her arm up and down, the pestle bumped noisily against the sky. From his home in the heavens, Onyame was driven mad by this constant banging. To get some peace and quiet he moved upwards so the sky became separated from the land.

Asase Yaa hoped she would be able to heal their relationship. She started to balance bowls beneath her, one on top of the other, so she could reach Onyame's home in the sky. When she had nearly made it, she cried out to her children for one more bowl, but there were none left. In desperation, she said, "Take one from the bottom and pass it to me." As her child pulled out the lowest bowl, the whole tower came crashing down. And so the sky and earth remain forever out of reach.

TELLING THE TRUTH

The Akan have complete trust in Asase Yaa. When a person is accused of lying, the village must 'ask the old woman'. This means the accused person has to bend down and touch the tip of their tongue to the earth. Just like an all-seeing mother, Asase Yaa will test their honesty and can work out if someone is telling even a small lie.

Asase Yaa owned a powerful sword that could be commanded to fight by itself. One day, her trickster son, the spider god Anansi, stole the sword and took it to Onyame, saying he would use it to protect the sky god. When an enemy army approached, Anansi ordered the sword to fight, but Anansi did not know the command to stop it. The sword turned on Onyame's own army and eventually, with no one else to kill, it slew the spider god himself. Asase Yaa's sword can only be wielded by the goddess of truth.

A gold-weight sword made from brass, Ghana, AD 1700–1900

SHAPING BELIEF

Asase Yaa is there at the very beginning and end of life as the guide who takes the dead to the Otherworld. It is traditional to raise and lower a coffin into the ground three times to make sure the goddess knows that it's entering the earth. In Ghana, symbols, known as *adinkra*, are used on clothing and pottery to represent important ideas. Asase Yaa's symbol represents the weight of the earth, the gravity that holds us to its surface, and the earth mother's love for all creation.

Thursday is her sacred day. To allow the goddess some rest, no one will work the fields or bury the dead on that day. She doesn't have temples dedicated to her. Instead she is honoured in the fields where every week gifts are left for her to enjoy on her day off.

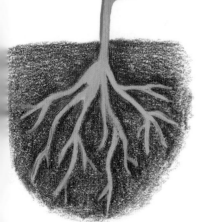

During the transatlantic slave trade in the 1800s, Asase Yaa was one of the gods to have been acknowledged by enslaved Akan. Today she is also worshipped in Jamaica, where many Akan settled. As her stories have travelled the oceans, she's given hope to many that there is a loving mother watching over them.

GAIA

Greek Earth Mother of All Life

FIRST MOTHER OF GODS

When the ancient Greeks asked how life on earth began, they decided that it all started with a goddess – Gaia. According to the legendary Greek writer Hesiod, Gaia was one of the first gods to emerge from the nothingness of Khaos.

Out of nothing Gaia produced Ouranos – the sky – to cover her on every side. She was so powerful she then created the mountains and the sea. After her came the depths of the Underworld, Tartaros, but also the hope of love, Eros. So, at the very beginning there was only Gaia, goddess of the earth, Ouranos, the god of the sky, the realm of the dead and the essence of love.

Together Gaia and Ouranos began to bring living beings into existence. First she gave birth to the powerful Titans, who were the family of gods and goddesses that ruled heaven and earth before the gods and godesses who ruled from Mount Olympus.

She also gave birth to the one-eyed giants called Cyclops and the hundred-handed, fifty-headed creatures known as Hecatoncheires. But their father, Ouranos, hated these monstrous children and wanted to get rid of them. He hid them inside Gaia's body, causing her immense pain and suffering. This is when Gaia started to challenge those around her.

REBEL GODDESS

Aching with pain from the creatures trapped inside her, Gaia created a sharp blade from a piece of diamond-like rock. She called her youngest and most bloodthirsty son, Kronus, one of the Titans, and asked him to stand guard until his father arrived. When Kronus saw Ouranos approach his mother, he grabbed the blade and attacked his father.

As Ouranus's blood spilled out, Gaia used it to create giants, nymphs and other supernatural beings. The goddess Aphrodite was said to have been created when part of Ouranus's body fell into the sea. Because of this, the sky god could not produce any more children and it looked as though Gaia had stopped him causing her and her children more pain.

A jug with Gaia painted on its body, Greece, 470–460 BC

But now it was her son Kronus's turn to wreak havoc. He had heard a prophecy that eventually his power would be challenged by his own children. To stop this, he swallowed each of his babies as soon as they were born. His wife, Rhea, was devastated as every single baby was snatched away from her and devoured by their father. Finally, and with Gaia's help, she hatched a cunning plan.

After she gave birth to her last child, Rhea took a stone and wrapped it in cloth so it looked like a baby. Kronus did as he always did, swallowing the baby-shaped bundle in one gulp. But Rhea had actually left her son, Zeus, with his grandmother. Gaia had defied Kronus, and she had saved Zeus from the terrible fate suffered by his other brothers and sisters, who were eventually rescued and ruled as the senior Olympian gods.

With Gaia's help, Zeus went on to defeat her other children, the Titans, and became chief of the gods. Gaia created human beings from the blood of the Titans and humankind began. Gaia had rebelled, first against her husband and then against her son, but she'd only done so out of protective love.

SHAPING BELIEF

Although Gaia is seen as mother of all life on earth, she is also worshipped as a goddess of death. She may have been honoured for over 6,000 years around the sacred site of Delphi in Greece, known as 'the belly-button of the world'. The Roman equivalent to Gaia was Terra. It is from her we get all terms referring to the earth, like *extraterrestrial*, which means 'outside the planet'. As a mother goddess and powerful female, she lies at the root of all creation and is still honoured by many today who see her as a source of inspiration.

EVE

First Woman Made by God

COMPANION AND EQUAL

The three main religions that grew out of the Middle East – Judaism, Christianity and Islam – all begin their creation stories with a man and a woman made by God. In the Christian tradition Eve is the first person to choose free will and independence. But she has also been seen as disobedient and deceptive.

The Genesis story in the Bible describes how the universe was created and the story has two very different parts. First God creates the heavens, earth, all creatures, man and woman in six days, then rests on the seventh day. In this part of the story, man and woman appear to be created equal. They were made at the same time and have the same rights to control all animals, birds and fish.

The second part of the story is where humankind gets into trouble. It starts with a lonely Adam, crafted from dust by God, who breathed life into him. He is placed in a beautiful paradise called the Garden of Eden, surrounded by wondrous trees, plants and animals that he has to look after. At the very centre of the garden God planted the 'Tree of Knowledge of Good and Evil' and told Adam he should never, ever eat its fruit. If he did, he would die. But Adam didn't want to be alone in paradise. He wanted a partner. So God took one of the man's rib bones as he slept. From this rib God made a woman, Eve, and brought her to Adam as his companion.

A Bible showing Adam and Eve in the Garden of Eden, England, 1607

FORBIDDEN FRUIT

Among the many creatures in the garden, God had created the serpent, which was craftier than any other beast. Whispering to Eve, it told her that she would not die if she ate the fruit of the Tree of Knowledge. Instead she would be like God and would know good and evil. Wanting this wisdom, Eve picked the forbidden fruit and ate it.

She then passed it to Adam, who also took a bite. Instantly they felt ashamed of being naked – something they hadn't noticed in their innocence before. They made clothes from fig leaves and when they heard God approaching, they hid from him in the trees. They now both had the knowledge of good and evil.

God knew right away that they had eaten the fruit. He accused Adam first, who blamed Eve. Then Eve blamed the serpent, saying it had tricked her. Disappointed at their betrayal, God cursed each of them in turn. He said the serpent must always crawl on its belly in the dust, and Adam would always have to work hard on the land. Everything he had so easily received in Eden would now be difficult to farm and grow.

Then God punished Eve too. He ordered that women would forever experience pain in childbirth. With that, Adam and Eve were banished from the garden and fierce angels with burning swords were placed around the Tree of Knowledge so that no one would ever eat its fruit again.

SHAPING BELIEF

In the Hebrew language, Eve is known as Hawwah, which means 'source of life' or 'living one'. As the first woman created, all humans are descended from her. Like the famous Pandora opening the box containing all the evils of the world in Greek mythology, by tasting the fruit Eve unlocked all the bad things humans experience, like shame and guilt. But she also allowed humans to become independent from God. Eve may have been tricked by the serpent, and harshly punished and criticised through the centuries as the very first sinner, but she was the original mother and her actions ultimately gave men and women free will.

MAWU

West African Creator of the Sun, the Moon and Life

LIFE ON EARTH

Among the Ewe and Fon people of Western Africa, creation centres around women. In Vodou belief, the creator Mawu appears in different versions of stories, but she's most often described as the daughter of Nana Buluku, who is the female supreme being, present at the beginning of existence. Nana Buluku had just one task – to create a god and goddess who could craft all life on earth. She made a son, Lisa, and a daughter, Mawu, although the two are so connected that they can be seen as just one being – Mawu-Lisa.

It wasn't up to Nana Buluku to make and manage life, so she retired to exist in peace and quiet. The hard work fell to Mawu-Lisa. Mawu is the moon, Lisa is the sun. Together they set about creating every aspect of the earth. They lovingly crafted each living creature out of clay and breathed life into them.

Some stories say that Mawu-Lisa had many children that would become responsible for all aspects of the world. Mawu's first daughter was called Gbadu and she controls fate and destiny. She sits on top of a palm tree and watches over everything happening on the earth, in the sea and in the sky. Gbadu plays an important role in one of Mawu's most interesting tales.

When Mawu made a monkey named Awe, she realised that his quick hands could be useful so she asked him to create other animals from clay. The bold monkey boasted to anyone that would listen that he had been given the role of a god and now he could breathe life into new creatures. He went around challenging Mawu and saying he was more powerful than her.

Gbadu, who was watching carefully, saw the chaos the monkey was spreading so sent one of her children to remind everyone that only her mother Mawu had the breath of life. Awe was angry so tried to prove he could make his clay rise up. He blew into it once – and failed. He blew in it twice – and still nothing happened. Eventually Mawu stepped in. To prove her point, she gave the monkey porridge made with the seeds of death. Only she had the power to make life and take it away.

COSMIC SERPENT AND RAINBOWS

In other creation stories it was a different animal that assisted Mawu – a very powerful snake named Aido-Hwedo. The snake has always existed and is part of the creative power that allowed Mawu to form life on earth. When Mawu travelled through the universe, this mystical serpent carried her in its mouth as her servant.

While creating all the creatures Mawu became concerned that the earth was becoming too heavy. She asked Aido-Hwedo to curl up beneath it and thrust it up into the sky. The snake holds the earth stable, as it turns around and around forever and it also ensures the movements of the stars in the sky. Whenever you see a rainbow, that's the cosmic serpent reflected in the heavens!

SHAPING BELIEF

Mawu is the creator of life and joy, holding all the knowledge and wisdom of the world. But she is also a protector of mothers and closely tied to all aspects of life and growth, rather than death and destruction. Her name comes from ma (not) and wu (kill) – so it literally means she does not kill.

In parts of West Africa and the Americas – as Vodou beliefs and practices travelled with enslaved people during the transatlantic slave trade – Mawu is seen as the life-giving force responsible for harvests.

When farmers sow their seeds, they may call on her to bring life into each one and give them a rich supply of food. There is a great deal of variety in how Mawu is understood. She can be a single creator, a male, a mix of both male and female, or more. But as a symbol of female creative energy she remains a powerful force that still inspires women today.

MOKOSH

Mother of the Earth, Slavic Goddess of Spinning and Fate

THE LIFE-GIVING EARTH

Have you ever heard of the seven great Slavic gods? They were worshipped long ago across Russia and Eastern and Central Europe before people started following the Christian religion. Mokosh, the Mother Goddess, was the only woman of the seven. She represents femininity, protection, good luck, wealth and a successful future. Her name is connected to moisture so she is seen as the source of nourishment for all life.

Mokosh is the earth mother who brings life through her waters, healing those in need. There are stories of miracles at her sacred wells, where the deaf could suddenly hear and the blind could suddenly see. She is an ancient goddess who has made the natural world rich and plentiful.

SPINNING TIME AND CONTROLLING DESTINY

In northern Russia, Mokosh is still honoured as a household spirit. She sometimes appears as a very tall woman with extremely long arms and a large head. As an earth goddess, she helps the people of the countryside by nourishing the grass to feed the sheep. She even helps farmers by shearing the sheeps' wool while they sleep. From this wool, she spins wonderful threads that she uses to weave precious garments. This is why she has been connected to fate. Like the strings of fortune Mokosh weaves a pattern, changing the course of the future by literally weaving the stories of peoples' lives.

As spinning and weaving are important crafts that Mokosh is connected to, she's sometimes shown like a spinning spider. Honouring her with offerings and prayers will keep her on your side until one day, at the end of life, like fate itself, she will cut the threads.

Mokosh is very protective of her followers. They believe that, by honouring her, they can learn to travel between worlds in trances and dreams. She is known as 'she who strikes with her wings' and the fact that she can fly reflects how powerful her worshippers can become.

If priestesses ever need help, they can ask Mokosh to protect them with her kindness and let them fly between different realms. She is also connected to butterflies, symbols of magical transformation, and bees, symbols of hard-working priestesses.

SHAPING BELIEF

Sometimes older goddesses were later transformed into Christian saints so that people could hold on to their special memories and traditions. As centuries passed, because of their shared protection of children and the vulnerable, Mokosh came to be associated with the Virgin Mary. She was also connected to Saint Parasceve, or 'Saint Friday'. On this day, women didn't have to work as hard as usual. They believed that if they swept the floors too heavily on a Thursday, it would cast dust into Mokosh's eyes the next day.

An embroidered Mokosh doll, Ukraine

Mokosh is still thought of as an important goddess today. You might see her embroidered on women's aprons as a sign that she protects those wearing her image. You might also see patterns connected to the goddess on strips of cloth tied to sacred birch or willow trees next to water – these are gifts asking for a rich harvest. As a loving mother, she makes the fields grow full, the water flow freely and brings healing and comfort to those that need her.

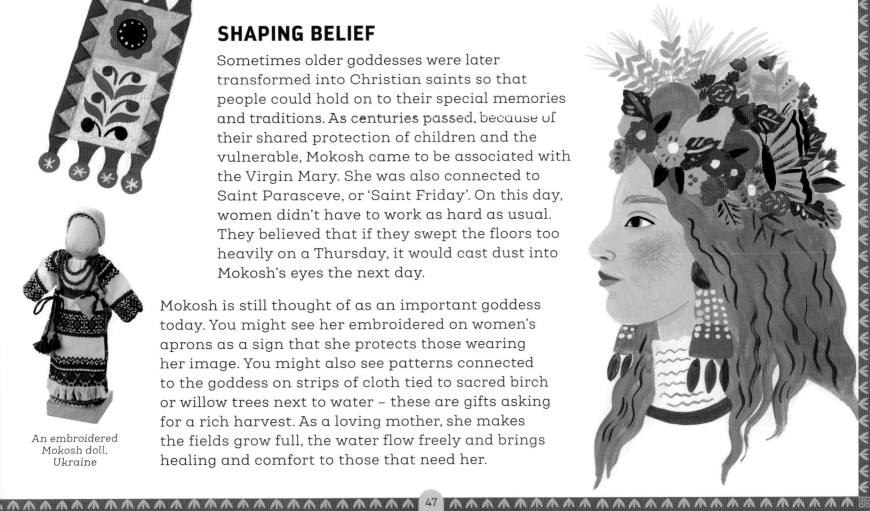

LILITH

Jewish Demon and Monster of the Night

DEMON SPIRIT

Lilith probably came from the female demons, or *lilitu*, of ancient Mesopotamia, which is today known as the Middle East. Demons were an important part of the religion of this area and although they could sometimes be kind, they were mainly dark, cruel spirits. Many clay tablets that have survived from thousands of years ago are carved with charms and spells to protect people against the harmful lilitu.

A magical gem engraved with Lilith, Mediterranean, AD 300–500

Working out exactly where Lilith comes from is complicated because her stories have changed over time and place. The earliest mention connects her to another powerful goddess – Inanna (see pages 8–9). In the story of Gilgamesh and the Huluppu Tree, Inanna had rescued the precious huluppu from being destroyed and replanted it in her sacred garden.

The tree soon became infested by a slithering snake that could not be charmed, an Anzu storm-bird who brought thunder and lightning and a female spirit called Lilith. Inanna cried out for help to protect the tree, so the famous hero Gilgamesh killed the snake living in its roots.

The Anzu bird then flew away to the mountain and Lilith escaped to the desert in terror. In this story, Lilith is shown as a harmful demon, destroying Inanna's life-giving tree.

THE FIRST WOMAN

Over 1,000 years later, Lilith takes a very different role in Jewish belief. She is the first wife of the first man – Adam. When they were created in the Garden of Eden, Adam said Lilith must always do exactly what he said. But strong, independent Lilith replied, "We are both equal because we are both created from the earth." Adam simply could not accept this. So, refusing to be weaker than her husband, Lilith called out God's secret name and flew away from the garden. Adam prayed for God's help to bring his wife back, so God sent three angels – Sanoi, Sansenoi and Semangloph – to track Lilith down. He told them: "If she wants to return, well and good. If not, she must accept that a hundred of her children will die every day."

The angels chased Lilith into the raging seas, threatening to drown her. When this didn't work, they pleaded with her to return, but still she refused, saying, "I was only created to sicken babies." She accepted God's word that some of her own children would die as punishment and began snatching other babies from their mothers. She then promised the three angels that whenever she saw their names written on an amulet, she would not take the baby it protected. She left with the fallen angel, Lucifer, and together they had many more demonic children who wreaked havoc among humans.

Lilith was said to fly in the dark of night, just like the owls she's often connected with. She could also transform her appearance and charm men. People often tried to guard themselves against Lilith's terror and many ancient objects have been found covered in magical protective spells. Special bowls would be placed upside down underneath a house to trap any demons and protect the family.

One ancient amulet includes this chilling message: "O you who fly in darkened rooms, Be off with you this instant, this instant, Lilith. You Thief, you breaker of bones."

SHAPING BELIEF

Lilith's curious connections with ancient demons and the Bible creation story have left her with a difficult reputation. For many thousands of years, people believed she caused the death of children and nightmares. This means she's usually remembered as a dark and evil demon. But because she stood up to her husband Adam and fought to be equal, Lilith is also seen by some as the symbol of female independence. While she's terrifying and deadly, she's also fascinating and powerful.

SEKHMET
Egyptian Lioness and Bringer of Destruction

A copper figure of Sekhmet, Egypt, about 664–332 BC

BORN FROM A CRY

Sekhmet is one of the oldest ancient Egyptian goddesses. Her name means 'the Powerful One', but she is described in many other ways too, including 'Lady of Slaughter', 'The Red Lady', 'Flame of the Sun' and 'Mistress of Dread'. She is sometimes called 'The Eye of Ra', because she represents the violent parts of her father, Ra, the sun god. Like him, she is often shown wearing a sun disc on her head. With the head of a lioness, she has the power of the fiercest hunter in Egypt and is a goddess of war but also of healing, so she has the power to both destroy and protect things.

One myth about the end of Ra's rule describes how Sekhmet came to be. Ra had carefully created heaven, earth, the gods and humankind, bringing law and order to his world. But again and again the people broke his rules and started to create chaos. In anger, Ra cried out for the help of the gentle mother goddess Hathor. She was the extremely powerful, positive and energetic goddess of dance, love, beauty and music. Hathor came to Ra's rescue but his rage soon turned her into 'The Powerful One' – the terrifying lioness-headed Sekhmet.

THIRSTY FOR BLOOD

Ra sent Sekhmet out into the desert and, with no understanding of kindness or sympathy, she destroyed everyone she met. Ra's anger had made her so thirsty for violence she drank human blood, rampaging through the desert, pulling people apart, ignoring their cries for mercy. The river Nile was soon stained red with spilled blood and, although she kept drinking it, she couldn't quench her thirst. By the end of her first day on earth, Sekhmet was bright red from head to foot. No one could stop her. Every sword that struck her, or arrow shot at her, broke into splinters when they touched Sekhmet's skin.

Ra soon realised that his punishment had gone too far. The people of Egypt had stopped breaking his rules. Instead they had come together to fight against this new terrible bloodthirsty danger. So Ra formed a cunning plan to stop Sekhmet in her tracks.

He ordered his people to collect huge amounts of red ochre from the island of Elephantine. He then told the powerful city of Heliopolis to mix massive vats of beer with the ground-down red stone. The liquid looked just like blood, so they filled up 7,000 urns and poured it into the field in front of the city.

As she rampaged towards Heliopolis, Sekhmet saw what looked like a field of blood. She gave out a huge roar and set about drinking every drop. But it wasn't blood and Ra's trick had worked. The beer soon made her completely drunk. She became peaceful and calm again, falling down on the streets of the city, and turning back into the beautiful cow-headed goddess Hathor. Just as Sekhmet had spread terror among the people, Hathor now began to spread love.

SHAPING BELIEF

In ancient Egypt a festival was held every year for Sekhmet. As the waters of the Nile turned red through churned up soil, people remembered her by drinking beer stained with pomegranate juice. They believed Sekhmet would protect them from flooding and destruction.

Her dangerous nature meant she was connected to disease and plagues, which could rage through populations, killing all in their path. But she was also thought of as a healing goddess who looked after doctors and medicine. She was often worshipped for protection against sickness and people carried amulets with her picture on to protect them against disease. As a symbol of female power, Sekhmet was a warrior goddess who could bring about both life and death with her hot, fiery breath and fierce strength.

DIANA

Roman Goddess of the Moon, the Hunt and Wild Animals

NOT BORN ON LAND

In ancient Roman stories, Diana is daughter of the sky god, Jupiter. She is a wild spirit, preferring the thrill of the hunt to romance. She never married, instead surrounding herself with friends that shared her love of adventure. Goddess of the outdoors, animals and the young, she knows her own mind, is physically and emotionally strong, and will give in to no one.

Even her birth goes against the norm. When Diana's mother, Latona, fell pregnant, Jupiter's wife was crazed with jealousy and made a powerful threat to punish her husband's lover. If the baby was born on firm land or under the bright sun, there would be trouble. Latona searched everywhere for a safe place to give birth. Eventually she found the floating island of Delos. It wasn't connected to the ocean floor, so it didn't count as 'firm land', and, hiding in the shade of an olive tree, she wasn't 'under the bright sun' either. There Latona gave birth to not one but two babies – the goddess Diana and her twin brother Apollo. They had escaped the curse!

As the twins grew, Diana and Apollo both became skilful hunters, remaining devoted to each other and their mother. One day, Niobe, queen of Thebes, proudly boasted that she was much better than Latona as she had given birth to 14 children instead of just two. Desperate to defend their mother's reputation, Diana killed all seven of Niobe's daughters, while Apollo killed the seven sons, piercing them with poisoned arrows. In revenge Diana had proved she was queen of the hunt.

GUARDIAN OF WILD PLACES

Diana's bow and arrows play an important part in her role as a huntress. With dogs by her side and a quiver of arrows, she often hunted in the woods. Many animals, including deer, were sacred to Diana and she was guardian of the countryside.

One sweltering hot day, she took a break from the hunt to bathe in a secret grotto with her nymph friends. But Diana wasn't the only one hunting in the woods that day. Hearing splashing water, a young hunter named Actaeon stumbled into the clearing. He peered over a rock to see where the women's voices were coming from and, for just a second, he saw the goddess completely naked.

The nymphs screamed in shock and tried to cover Diana. No mortal man could look on the body of a goddess! Diana was furious. At first she wanted to shoot Actaeon but instead she splashed some magical water on his face. As soon as it touched him, fur began to grow over his body. Antlers emerged from his head and hooves appeared where his feet had been.

A gold coin showing Diana, Italy, 145–161

In no time at all he had transformed completely into a stag. Frightened, Actaeon ran off blindly into the wood, but his own hunting dogs caught his scent and tracked him down. The goddess had her revenge.

SHAPING BELIEF

Such a mighty huntress was the perfect protector of unmarried young women in the ancient world. She led girls from childhood to adulthood, seeing them through the big transformations in a woman's life. Driven by a wild energy and keen to prove she was as strong and capable as any man, Diana is still often associated with the moon, which is as changeable and fascinating as the goddess herself.

FREYJA

Norse Goddess of Love, War and Magic

NO ONE'S FOOL

Of all the women in the Norse or 'Viking' religion, Freyja is one of the most important. Wherever the Vikings reached on their extraordinary longships, the goddess and her stories travelled with them.

Symbolic of love, springtime, beauty, gold and magic, Freyja is fearless, feisty and temperamental. She's also a woman at home on the battlefield. She moves among the dead, and her assistants – the feared female Valkyries – choose half of all the warriors killed in battle to live with her in the Field of the People, known as Folkvang.

Freyja can travel across the Nine Realms on her chariot pulled by two dark grey cats. Or she rides her powerful boar, Hildisvini. She also has a cloak of falcon feathers that allows her to fly.

A silver pendant representing Freyja, Sweden, 800–1099

Freyja is so beautiful that she is constantly being pestered by men who want to marry her. In one story she is almost tricked into marrying Thrym, the king of the giants. Freyja gave her feathered cape to the trouble-making god, Loki, so he could sneak into Thrym's court and uncover his plans. Once inside, Loki discovered that the giant had stolen the magical hammer of the thunder god Thor and would only return it if Freyja married him.

They hatched a plan to get it back, but when Loki and Thor told Freyja to dress for her wedding to the thieving giant, she began to shake with fury. The halls of the gods trembled beneath her and her precious necklace broke off from her neck. They couldn't make her marry a troll king!

Since Freyja would not be moved, Thor and Loki settled on another plan instead. Thor, the enormous god of thunder, dressed in Freyja's clothes, put on her necklace and went in her place.

When he started swallowing animals whole and emptying huge casks of mead, Thrym began to suspect that perhaps this wasn't the beautiful goddess Freyja after all. Realising he had been discovered, Thor tore off Freyja's clothes, grabbed his hammer and killed all around him. When everyone was dead, Freyja retrieved her necklace, which was more precious to her than anything else.

LOVER OF GOLD

Freyja loves gold so much that she cries solid tears of it. Her necklace, Brisingamen, which was forged from fire by four dwarfs, appears in another of her most famous stories. Freyja had gone behind the back of Odin, chief of the gods, to get the necklace and he wanted to know about her treachery. So he instructed Loki to investigate.

Loki went to spy on Freyja, but she had sealed her door tight. Turning himself into a fly he squirmed through a crack in the roof. Then he changed into a flea and bit Freyja on the cheek. As she rolled over, he slipped off the necklace and took it straight to Odin.

Furious at this deception, Freyja stormed to the great hall and demanded Odin return her treasure. He refused. Instead he punished her for keeping secrets, ordering her to stir up war and misery among the people of earth. She agreed, war followed, and Freyja once again got her necklace back.

SHAPING BELIEF

Freyja was also worshipped as goddess of magic because she was the first to use *seiðr*, which is a type of magic practised in Scandinavia that changed the path of fate, altering the present and the future. This form of magic was particularly associated with women and, as such, women who practised it became some of the most powerful figures in Viking society.

IZANAMI

Japanese Goddess of Death and New Life

RITUAL OF LOVE

The Japanese Shinto goddess Izanami has a complicated relationship with life and death. She created all existence but was eventually killed giving birth to the god of fire. She then descended into the Underworld as a guardian of the dead. Life and death are always finely balanced, as Izanami's story shows.

As the first beings, Izanami and her husband Izanagi had to start creation. With the help of a heavenly jewelled spear, they stood on the floating bridge between heaven and earth, stirring the sea below. Drops of salty water dripped from the end of the spear and created an island called Onogoroshima. The god and goddess came down from the heavens and made this place their home.

There, Izanami and Izanagi built a grand palace with a pillar at the centre. When they decided to have children, they performed a ritual around this pillar, where Izanami went round one side and her husband went around the other. When they met, Izanami welcomed Izanagi with joy and she became pregnant.

Soon after she gave birth to a child. Sadly he had no bones and was known as Hiruko, or 'leech child'. The parents cast Hiruko away in a boat, but fortunately he could swim. He grew strong and became the god of fishermen. In the story, the couple went on to perform the ritual around the pillar again and this time Izanami gave birth to many more gods and the eight islands of Japan. She is mother on earth and in heaven.

DEATH AND DARKNESS

However, of all the children Izanami had given birth to, none of them represented fire. So she became pregnant one more time to bring a fire god into the world. But while the baby grew inside her, it began to burn and flame. Izanami became very sick and, finally, as the baby left her body like a volcano erupting, she died.

Izanagi was devastated at the loss of his wife and determined to find her in the Underworld. As he walked into the land of darkness, he could see absolutely nothing. Izanami heard him calling out to her, saying he'd come to take her home. She replied that she had already eaten the food of the dead, which meant she could never leave.

A shrine containing small statues of 30 Shinto kami, Japan, 1600s

But Izanagi didn't give up. He would do anything to bring his wife back. He took the comb from his hair and lit it to make a torch. Izanami appeared, terrifying in the flickering light. Rotting and covered in maggots, she had already been transformed by death. Izanami chased after Izanagi as he fled, horrified, to the entrance. She set the warriors of the Underworld on him, and they pursued him, screaming and shouting, desperate to keep him in the land of the dead.

Finally Izanagi reached the light. He rolled a rock across the opening, shutting earth off from the dead for eternity. Izanami screamed from behind the rock that she would take 1,000 lives every day as revenge. Izanagi replied that he would create 1,500 each day so that life could continue.

SHAPING BELIEF

The story of Izanami's life – and death – taps into some of the most important questions we ask ourselves as humans: How did we get here? Where do we go when we die? Izanami was one of the first *kami*, or protective spirits of the Shinto religion. These spirits represent the features and forces of nature and many people believe that Izanami's tale can provide them with answers and guidance through life.

ANAT

Middle Eastern Goddess of War and Peace

THIRSTY FOR WAR

Three major world religions grew out of the Middle East – Judaism, Christianity and Islam. People who follow these religions worship just one god, but we know that their ancestors in this area, including the Canaanites mentioned in the Bible, worshipped many deities. One of the most important Middle Eastern goddesses, worshipped around 4,000 years ago, was Anat. Her stories were recorded on ancient clay tablets.

Anat is passionate about everything, including violence. She is an extremely beautiful woman who is often shown with animal features – cow horns and bird wings, which she uses to zoom around at great speed. As the daughter of El, the supreme god, Anat has many siblings. Among these are three brothers: Baal, the god of storms, who she loves dearly, Yam, god of the swirling seas, and Mot, god of death, who she hates.

In one story, her brother Yam was hungry for power. He told their father that he wanted to take over as king of all the gods. El asked Anat to make preparations for a fabulous coronation ceremony, but she had other plans. Instead she encouraged her beloved brother Baal to fight Yam for the right to be ruler.

They soon became locked in a vicious battle. Yam launched an army of sea creatures at his brother. But Baal, who had two magical clubs, managed to pound Yam to death. Now that he had ultimate power, Baal wanted a magnificent palace fit for a king. In devotion to her favourite brother, Anat travelled to see their father El, to demand he build a suitably spectacular court.

With earthquakes shaking around her, Anat cursed El. She threatened that his hair would flow with blood if he didn't do what she said. Eventually she got her way and Baal was built the most incredible home. Sitting proudly on his throne he announced that every other god had to recognise him as king. Only one refused – his brother Mot, the god of death.

A BATTLE WITH DEATH

Now Baal had another fight on his hands. Mot, the terrifying Lord of the Underworld, dragged him down to his realm and killed him. Anat was devastated. She clawed at her skin and never-ending tears drenched her face. In anger she charged into Mot's kingdom and grabbed him, screaming, "Where is my brother?" Mot replied that he had crushed Baal in his jaws.

Angry and seeking revenge, Anat attacked Mot, slashing him with her sword. Even that was not enough for her – she wanted to reduce him to dust. She burned his body, ground up the ash and scattered it across the fields so Mot could never return. As Mot died, Baal came back to life. Anat could not believe this miracle and hugged her dear brother, still covered in the blood of Mot. As a sign of her bloodthirsty nature the goddess is often described as wearing a necklace of skulls and a skirt made from human hands.

SHAPING BELIEF

Anat's ability to destroy people – and sometimes even whole towns – in rage has meant she has always been connected with war and battle. Ancient arrowheads inscribed with the words 'Son of Anat' have been discovered, which suggest that this title was an honour among warriors.

While she is best known for her connection to war, she is also celebrated for bringing its opposite – peace. Her stories spread to ancient Egypt, where the Pharaoh Rameses II named one of his children Bintanath, meaning 'Daughter of Anat', in her honour. It remains a popular name in Israel. Now more people are seeking out stories and images of this ancient goddess as a fascinating example from the past of powerful females who could fight to get what they wanted.

Limestone engraved with Anat, Egypt, 1292–1189 BC

HEL
Norse Guardian of the Underworld

THE ROAD TO HEL

Hel is the only daughter of the Norse trouble-making god, Loki, and the giantess Angrboda. She is guardian of the underworld realm that shares her name and her brothers are the world-serpent Jörmungandr and the wolf Fenrir. But while they take animal forms, Hel is a human woman with a fierce-looking face.

Concerned that Loki's three children would cause trouble in the future, chief of the gods Odin decided to separate them. They bound the wolf in strong chains and hurled the world-serpent into the sea, where it forever bites its own tail and wraps around the world. Then Odin gave Hel an important job – she was to provide a home to all those that died of sickness or old age.

In the Viking period, the universe was sometimes described as having Nine Realms, all held in the branches of a sacred tree, Yggdrasill. Humans live on Midgard and the gods live in Asgard. Heroes feast for eternity in Valhalla and Hel is guardian of the dead who live in Niflheim, a land of mist and shadows.

Hel lives in Helheim in a huge mansion where countless zombie-like servants treat her as mistress of the dead. She eats her food from a plate called 'Hunger' and cuts it with a knife called 'Famine'. While she feasts, those around her starve.

At the centre of Hel's kingdom is a bubbling, boiling spring of water, protected by a dragon. This is the source of all life and everything will eventually return to it. The great rivers all flow out of Hel's realm, which is surrounded by high walls. The gates of Niflheim are protected by a huge blood-stained hound called Garm.

MISTRESS OF THE DEAD

Hel plays an important part in the death of the heroic god Baldr. He was the most loved son of Odin and Frigg, but while he was a child his mother dreamed he would be killed. Terrified, she gave him powers that meant that any object thrown at him would simply bounce off. The only thing she forgot to include was mistletoe. One day when the gods were having fun throwing missiles and watching them fly off Baldr, Loki tried something different. He made a spear of mistletoe, gave it to Baldr's blind brother and told him to throw it through the air. It hit Baldr and killed him, at which point he was taken to Hel's kingdom to live among the dead.

Hel kept the hero with her, but Baldr's mother could not live without him. She asked one of his brothers to ride on Odin's eight-legged horse and beg Hel for her son back. Hel met the messenger and listened to the devastated mother's plea. Thinking carefully, she made a pledge. If all creatures, alive or dead, wept together for Baldr then she would let him return. But if just one person refused to cry then he would stay with her forever.

While everyone grieved for their lost god, one woman alone didn't shed a tear. Could this woman be Loki in disguise? With this Hel managed to keep Baldr with her and he would not return again until the end of the world.

SHAPING BELIEF

The name Hel comes from an old Norse word meaning 'to cover' so it is probably a reference to being buried after death. You might wonder if the Christian word 'Hell' comes from the name of her deathly kingdom. In fact, the two are very different. Hel is icy and cold, while Hell is fiery and hot.

Hel is most often associated with the dead and that's why she's shown half-living and half-decaying like a corpse. Her realm is not particularly pleasant, but it's not a place of torture and horror either – it's a place where all the people that were not heroes or warriors in life end up after death.

RANGDA

Bali's Queen of Demons and Widow-Witch

WITCH AND WARRIOR

On the Indonesian island of Bali most people practise a form of Hinduism that honours unique gods and goddesses that are not found anywhere else. They also believe in a set of demons that are truly terrifying, known as the *Leyak*.

These creatures walk around in the day in human form. But by night their frightful faces have huge bulging eyes, wide fangs and long red lolling tongues. Their heads tear away from their bodies, trailing their insides behind them, and they fly around searching for victims.

The Leyak have a thirst for human blood, particularly that of pregnant women and newborn babies. They haunt graveyards and feed on corpses. They can also shape-shift, taking on the form of animals. This means they are very hard to discover. The queen of the Leyak is called Rangda. She leads all demons and is both feared and honoured. There's no mistaking that Rangda is a terrifying goddess. She has long claws and wild hair that falls to her waist.

Rangda is an important part of the universal forces that many Balinese people believe either come from heaven or the Underworld. Together these forces form an orderly universe. One force without the other causes chaos, so they need to be kept in balance through rituals. The protective mythical creature Barong balances the destructive forces of Rangda. She can be both protective and destructive, so Rangda does not only cause problems, she removes them too.

This magical witch Rangda has roots in real women from the past. In one story, 1,000 years ago there lived a princess called Mahendradatta. Her husband, the king, discovered she was practising black magic and sent her away to the jungle where she became bitter and angry. When her husband died, Mahendradatta was left a widow, which is where the name Rangda comes from – it means 'widow' in ancient Balinese.

Her son Airlangga became king, but he left his mother pining alone in the jungle. She wanted revenge against her son and the people that had exiled her, so she summoned all the demons of the wild, the Leyaks and spirits that caused disease, then sent a plague down on the kingdom. Half the people in the country died.

Eventually King Airlangga called on the protective Barong, who is also known as the Great Lord, and there was an epic battle. Ever since, this historical woman Mahendradatta has been connected to Rangda because she was a widow-witch and controlled an army of demons.

MAGICAL MOTHER

A different version of the story also involves the dangerous widow, this time known as Calon Arang. She was a black magician and had a very beautiful daughter. Everyone in their village was so afraid of her that no one wanted to marry her daughter, which made Calon Arang angry.

To punish the villagers, she took one of their children – a young girl – to the cemetery, killed her as a sacrifice and released a curse. First a flood destroyed the village, then those who survived became sick and died. Calon Arang wreaked havoc with a magic scroll that gave her incredible power.

A carved wooden Rangda mask, Bali, about 1950

Armies were sent in to defeat her, but she was too powerful. Eventually the king realised that Calon Arang would only be happy if someone worthy married her daughter, so he arranged a wedding with his handsome, brave adviser.

Exhausted after seven days and nights of wedding celebrations, Calon Arang fell into a deep sleep. Her new son-in-law sneaked into her bedroom and stole the magic scroll. Calon Arang was now weakened and after a fierce battle she eventually died.

SHAPING BELIEF

In Bali, some temples have masks and costumes of Rangda that are worn during special religious festivals. As part of a ritual to keep opposite forces balanced – like night and day, life and death, happiness and sadness – people put on performances of the epic battle between Rangda and Barong. It's performed differently in different parts of Bali, but the outcome is always a draw – neither god wins or loses and each one can only exist alongside the other.

MEDUSA

Snake-Haired Demon with Deadly Eyes

PUNISHMENT AND REVENGE

People have told stories of Medusa for over 2,000 years. With snakes for hair and a wild, staring gaze that turned people to stone, she is remembered as the evil demon who was eventually beheaded by the ancient Greek hero Perseus.

Medusa was one of three mythical sisters and together they were known as the Gorgons. Her sisters, Stheno and Euryale, were immortal, which meant Medusa was the only one that could ever be killed. In one story, Medusa was a beautiful woman who became hideous-looking when Athena cursed her. Athena was enraged because the god of the sea, Poseidon, had seduced Medusa in one of her sacred shrines. This was disrespectful towards Athena so, as punishment, she transformed the young maiden into a monster.

A MONSTER AND A MIRROR

The story of Medusa's dramatic death is one of the most famous and thrilling in all Greek mythology. It started with King Polydectes wanting to marry Perseus's mother Danae. Polydectes knew Perseus would do anything to protect his mother, so he hatched a plan to send the hero far away. He set Perseus the challenge of bringing him the head of Medusa – an impossible mission.

But, bold and boasting, Perseus agreed. On his way, he had help from the gods and goddesses. Hermes, god of travel, gave him a pair of golden winged sandals. Hades, god of the Underworld, gave him an invisibility helmet. Hephaestus, god of blacksmiths, gave him a sword and Athena, still full of hatred for Medusa, gave him a mirrored shield.

Perseus found Medusa sleeping in a cave. He wore the helmet and winged sandals so he could quickly get away. Using the shield like a mirror, he could see where he was going without looking into Medusa's deadly stare. Once he had crept as close as he could, he struck out with his sword. With one swipe, the head of the snake-haired monster fell to the floor. But then, something unexpected happened. Nobody knew that Medusa had been pregnant and, as she died, Poseidon's child – a winged horse called Pegasus – flew out of her neck.

A bronze head of Medusa, Italy, about 50–75 BC

Perseus quickly threw Medusa's head into a bag and escaped, her two sisters chasing after him. But Medusa's power continued long after her death. On his travels, Perseus stopped to rescue a beautiful woman named Andromeda from a dangerous sea serpent. After bravely battling the monster, he laid down Medusa's head. Her blood turned the seaweed to stone and formed the red corals of the sea.

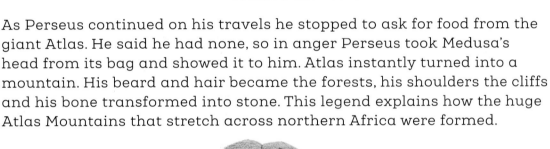

As Perseus continued on his travels he stopped to ask for food from the giant Atlas. He said he had none, so in anger Perseus took Medusa's head from its bag and showed it to him. Atlas instantly turned into a mountain. His beard and hair became the forests, his shoulders the cliffs and his bone transformed into stone. This legend explains how the huge Atlas Mountains that stretch across northern Africa were formed.

SHAPING BELIEF

Sometimes Medusa is shown as beautiful and sometimes she is monstrous and demonic, with the tusks of a boar, a wide lolling tongue and even a bristly beard. But two things never change – her writhing, venomous snake hair and wide staring eyes that turn things to stone. In ancient Greece, images of Medusa were placed outside buildings to protect people from danger. So although she suffered a terrible death, she was also given an important role as a guardian. And whatever happened to her severed head? Well, Athena placed it in the centre of her breastplate of course.

KALI

Hindu Goddess of Time, Creation and Destruction

TIME TRAVELLER

Kali is known by many names, including 'She Who is Death', 'Origin of and Devourer of All Things' and 'The Force of Time'. She is a warrior, happiest on the battlefield where she carries fearsome weapons, beheads demons and defeats the forces of chaos. Hindus believe that the universe is created over and over again. We are living in the Age of Kali – Kali is time. There are different versions of how she first appeared, but in each case she wasn't actually born. Instead, most often, she bursts out of the forehead of the warrior goddess, Durga (see pages 26–27).

One story tells how Durga was fighting two terrible demons, Chanda and Munda. Riding into battle on a lion, Durga became so angry with the demons that her uncontrollable rage exploded out of her head in the form of a thin, terrifying black figure. This was Kali.

Nobody could match Kali's fierce strength or power and, sending out a blood-chilling cry, she defeated the two demons, cutting their heads from their bodies. She delivered the severed heads to Durga and the battle was won.

DEVOURER OF DEATH

In another tale, the gods and goddesses were fighting another dangerous enemy called Raktabija. They were losing, and victory seemed impossible, because with every single drop of Raktabija's blood that touched the ground, another demon sprang up in its place. The awful army would not stop growing until Kali, destroyer of evil, appeared on the battlefield.

She spread out her huge red tongue, catching the drops of blood before they hit the earth. She then gobbled up Raktabija and his army of demons and danced uncontrollably to celebrate. These stories can make Kali seem scary, but while she is connected with death and destruction, she also represents life and love.

Kali has an important relationship with the god Shiva. He is the calm to her storm. She is wild, passionate and represents the female energies that move the universe, known as *Shakti*, while he remains still and quiet. When she began dancing with joy after battle, Kali nearly killed Shiva by stomping on his chest, until he managed to calm her down.

But one cannot exist without the other and together they show the important relationship between energetic action and gentle thought that is needed to keep balance in the universe. Like the complicated world she represents, Kali has a beautiful, kind side, but also a dangerous, destructive one.

A stone figure of Kali, India, 1700s

SHAPING BELIEF

Kali has black skin, which is sometimes shown as blue, and four arms holding weapons and the heads of those she has defeated. She is often naked or dressed in a skirt made from human arms. She wears a necklace of skulls, which represents all the things that Kali destroyed in her quest to reach the highest spiritual state. They are not just the heads of people she has killed in battle, they are a sign that she has moved to a deeper understanding of life. Kali is one of the most important Hindu goddesses because she is seen as the mother of the universe. In fact, Kali is the universe, the never-ending cycle of time – life, death and all that is wonderful and terrifying about it.

MARY

Highest Among Women in Christianity and Islam

HOLY BIRTH

For thousands of years, Mary has been honoured across the world as one of the most important sacred women, although her stories are different depending on whether she's being honoured by Christians or Muslims. In Christianity, many people believe she has miraculous powers to heal and her son is Jesus, the son of God. As his mother, Mary is the holiest of women and has many names including 'Ever Pure', 'Our Lady' and 'Queen of Heaven'. In Islam, she is called Maryam, 'Tahira' or 'Pure of Heart' and her son is the prophet Isa, peace be upon him, one of God's messengers.

Mary's life is recorded by Christians as beginning with her parents, Joachim and Anne. They were struggling to have a baby. One day, an angel wondrously appeared to the couple and told them they would have a child who would be spoken about throughout the land. From that moment on her parents knew Mary was going to be special.

Artwork based on Christian beliefs

Her best-known story from the Christian Bible tells how Mary miraculously became pregnant with the son of God. Just like her mother years before, one day an angel appeared to Mary. The Angel Gabriel saw she was scared, so calmed her by saying, "Do not be afraid." He then told Mary that she would give birth to a son and she should call him Jesus. Mary was very confused, but the angel explained that the father would not be Joseph, the carpenter she was engaged to, it would be God himself. Despite her fear, Mary replied, "I am the Lord's servant," and so she became pregnant.

SEEKING SAFETY

Life would have been very scary for Mary. She wasn't yet married to Joseph and now, all of a sudden, she was pregnant. Joseph soon found out about the baby and thought he might quietly end their relationship. But, yet another angel visited him in a dream and told him they should stay together. It wasn't going to be easy. Emperor Augustus had issued a census, which meant Joseph had to return to where he was born to register. Together they set off on a long journey across the country. Heavily pregnant, poor and frightened, Mary rode on a donkey all the way back to Bethlehem where she gave birth to Jesus in a stable. In Islam, the story is similar, except Mary made the trip to Bethlehem with her uncle and gave birth next to a palm tree, from which she ate some fresh dates to help relieve the pain.

A painted icon of the Virgin Mary and child, Russia, 1820–1830

Meanwhile, the Christian story continues as King Herod hears a worrying prophecy. The message said that there was now a baby in his city who would one day have greater power than him. To get rid of this danger, he ordered all newborn babies to be killed. He sent soldiers charging through the streets, tearing crying babies from their mothers' arms.

To protect their son, Mary and Joseph fled to Egypt, only returning home when they knew he would be safe.

An ivory statue of Mary and child, France, 1325–1350

SHAPING BELIEF

The protective love Mary felt for her child has always inspired artists. In Christianity, she is usually shown as a strong, caring mother, cradling baby Jesus, but sometimes she is shown to be crushing evil beneath her feet. By bringing her son into the world, Mary became a symbol of the Christian church and people pray to her as a way of speaking to God and Jesus about their troubles. Around the world, there have been many stories of Mary visiting worshippers. In 1858, in the town of Lourdes in southern France, a poor young girl called Bernadette was gathering firewood, when Mary miraculously appeared to her.

She had been sent from God as a messenger, so an important holy shrine was built where healing ceremonies began to take place and people could communicate with God.

Honoured in both Christianity and Islam, people travel from far and wide to visit her holy shrines. Christians believe that Mary protects the poor, the weak and the vulnerable and, for Muslims, Maryam's story of hardship provides love, compassion and protection in times of need.

GUANYIN
Buddhist Goddess of Kindness and Mercy

A THOUSAND EYES, A THOUSAND ARMS

One of the most important goddesses in China, Guanyin protects the people that follow her. She can guard against fire, flood, storms, imprisonment, animal and demon attacks. She frees people from fear and anger, and can grant the prayers of women who want to have children. As the goddess who can hear the cries of people in need, her name means 'the one who can perceive the sounds of the world'. A faithful Buddhist, Guanyin achieved the state of enlightenment – the highest spiritual state. This meant she could leave the never-ending cycle of death and rebirth, known as *samsara*. Given this choice, Guanyin chose to remain on earth to help others reach enlightenment too.

In one story, Guanyin makes a promise never to rest until she has set all humans free from reincarnation – where a dead person's spirit returns to life in another body. She kindly listened out for cries for help, but so many humans were crying at once, she desperately struggled to hear them all. The deafening noise eventually split her head into eleven pieces. Amitabha Buddha, the great saviour, realised that Guanyin was trying to do good, so he gave her the gift of 1,000 eyes to watch out for the people suffering.

A bronze figure of Guanyin, China

Next time, when she saw so many desperate pleas, Guanyin tried to reach out her loving arms to each one. But she soon became exhausted and her arms shattered too. Once more Amitabha came to her rescue. He gave her 1,000 arms so she could offer help wherever it was needed.

TEACHER OF MYSTERIES

Another story tells how Guanyin found her faithful follower Shancai. Guanyin had been hiding on the rocky island of P'u-t'o when a young disabled boy heard that a mysterious great teacher might be able to help him learn Buddhist rules and wisdom.

Although it was a very difficult journey, Shancai persevered, eventually finding Guanyin on the island in the middle of the sea. After talking with the young boy, she decided to put him to the test. Quick as a flash, she conjured up an illusion of three angry pirates waving swords, who raced up from the sea and tried to attack Guanyin.

Shancai watched as the three figures chased down his beloved teacher. He couldn't run, but he had to help Guanyin somehow. He crawled to the cliff edge and threw himself off the side so he could reach her. But suddenly, as he was falling, he stopped in mid-air. Guanyin had decided he had passed her test of loyalty and she was happy to take him on as her student and teach him her secrets. As a reward she helped him to walk again and from then on Shancai never left her side.

SHAPING BELIEF

Guanyin is a kind and loving teacher, always providing support and wisdom to those that need it. Her mantra is 'om mani padme hum', which means 'the jewel is in the lotus'. She is usually shown wearing white and emerging from a lotus flower to symbolise her great wisdom. Man, woman, king, poor person, even a dragon – Guanyin is dedicated to teaching Buddhism to her followers and she does this by changing into any shape. She's incredibly popular across Asia and her image appears in many houses and public spaces, where she offers protection and love to all those she gazes down on. She has become associated with vegetarianism because of her compassion for all living things and she is seen as a calming, gentle guardian and guide.

ISIS

Ancient Egyptian Mother and Magician, Wisest of Women

A bronze aegis of Isis, Egypt, about 664–332 BC

A BROTHER'S REVENGE

Of all the ancient Egyptian goddesses Isis is one of the oldest and most well known. She came from a very powerful family – her father was Geb, god of the earth, and her mother was Nut, goddess of the sky (see pages 14–15). But Isis was important in her own right. One of the most famous ancient Egyptian stories describes her love and revenge for her husband and brother, Osiris, and the birth of her son Horus, the falcon-headed god of kings.

Isis and Osiris had a special relationship. As god of life and death, Osiris ruled fairly over Egypt, with Isis as his queen. He represented control and brought order to his lands while his brother, Set, represented chaos. Set was jealous of his brother's power and decided to play a cunning trick on him. Secretly he measured Osiris's body and made a beautiful wooden chest to fit him exactly. Then he invited all the gods to a grand banquet, promising that whoever fitted inside the chest could keep it. All the gods tried, but only Osiris fitted perfectly. Once he was inside, Set slammed down the lid, nailing it closed so Osiris was trapped. After being thrown into the river Nile and carried out to sea, eventually Osiris drowned inside the chest. But that wasn't enough for Set. He then cut Osiris's body into 42 pieces and scattered them throughout the kingdom of Egypt.

LOVE AND MAGIC

Isis pined so deeply for Osiris that she filled the Nile with her tears, flooding its banks. She searched everywhere for the parts of his body and, following a map given to her by the god of wisdom, Thoth, she finally collected each piece. As she lovingly put his body back together again, Isis became the first embalmer and her husband the first mummy. But she still needed to bring his soul back from the land of the dead. Sending a secret message to her sister, Nephthys, the two women went to Osiris's temple and began to cast powerful healing spells. Their magic brought Osiris back to life and Isis fell pregnant with his true heir to the throne, Horus.

Meanwhile, Set still wanted control of Egypt. Isis knew he would be a danger to her child so she ran away to give birth to Horus, hiding in the papyrus marshes of the Nile. As Horus grew up, Isis had to protect him from his angry uncle, so she often disguised herself as a human.

She sometimes travelled with guards and in one story seven terrifying scorpion gods protected her. When a rich woman refused to help Isis, the scorpion gods were furious and stung the woman's son. Feeling sorry for the innocent boy, Isis cured him and gained a reputation as a kind, caring goddess who helped humans.

In another tale Isis tricked Ra, the most important sun god, into telling her his 'secret name'. She created a magical snake out of clay, brought it to life and ordered it to bite Ra. The poison almost killed him and only Isis could provide the cure. She said she would only help Ra if he revealed his true name, because this would give her and Horus an incredible amount of power. Eventually Ra gave in and Isis was able to gain the greatest influence among the gods.

SHAPING BELIEF

Isis was believed to be the most powerful magician in existence after she discovered Ra's secret name. As healer of the sick, protector of the poor and guardian of the people, Isis was greatly honoured far and wide. Temples were built to honour her all over the ancient world, from Britain to the Black Sea. She was popular because she represents many aspects of ancient Egyptian femininity: she was an ideal mother, a loving wife, a confident queen and she used her magical healing powers to control the very essence of life and death.

HECATE

Ancient Greek Goddess of Protection and the Spirit World

ABOVE GROUND, BELOW GROUND

Not much is known about the mysterious Greek goddess Hecate. What we do know is that she is constantly changing and taking on new forms. Often shown as a triple goddess – three versions of herself in one spirit – her powers over the earth, sea and heavens were given to her by her parents Perses, the Titan god of war, and Asteria, the Titaness of the stars.

Hecate was particularly honoured by Zeus, chief of the gods, and she's usually shown holding symbols – a torch to light the way, a dagger to protect travellers, and a rope or key to open doorways. She moved freely between earth and the Underworld, so people placed statues of her at crossroads or at the entrance to their houses to bring them good luck as they travelled from place to place.

Hecate is a goddess who guides people through life and shows them the way. Her black dog was her trusty companion. One myth says the dog is actually the Trojan queen Hecuba who went mad after seeing her children die in war. Crazed with sorrow, she began howling and barking, until finally she leaped into the sea where the gods transformed her. From then on people believed that whenever Hecate was near, they would hear the tragic howling of her dog.

GUIDE AND TORCHBEARER

Hecate plays an important part in one famous tale, where she helps to save Persephone, Zeus's daughter, from Hades, the god of the Underworld. Hades had fallen in love with Persephone and wanted to marry her. One day, as Persephone was walking through the fields, the ground suddenly opened up beneath her. Out burst Hades riding a horse-drawn chariot. He grabbed Persephone, took her back to his realm and claimed her as his wife.

As Persephone's mother, Demeter, desperately tried to find out what had happened, Hecate knew she could help. She had heard everything. She took Demeter to Helios, the sun god. He had seen everything. So thanks to Hecate and Helios, Demeter discovered the truth and worked out where her daughter had been taken.

Persephone wasn't allowed to eat while in the Land of the Dead, but eventually she gave in to her hunger and swallowed six pomegranate seeds. This was enough for Hades to keep her imprisoned with him for six months over the winter - one month for every seed. Thankfully, when springtime came, Persephone was finally released from the Underworld and Hecate became her constant companion, guiding her with flaming torches and keys on their journey between the two worlds.

SHAPING BELIEF

Hecate is sometimes seen as scary because of her dog companion and three forms, but her role is usually one of guidance, protection and light. She is hugely powerful and able to bring success and failure, yet she is not a terrifying or evil goddess.

Hecate is still popular among modern-day pagans, or Wicca, as she is honoured as a goddess of witchcraft. She's connected with poisonous plants and trees of death, and you'll often see her name written in spells on ancient curse tablets. Mysterious, magical, dark and light, Hecate is a goddess who can provide protection or bring about destruction.

A marble statue of Hecate, Diana and Selene, Rome, 161–200

SARASVATI

Hindu Goddess of Learning and the Arts

FLOWING WATER AND WORDS

Sarasvati is one of the oldest and most important goddesses in the Hindu religion. She represents wisdom, speech, music, art, inspiration and was said to have invented Sanskrit, the language that is at the very heart of the Hindu faith.

She is connected to the god of creation – Brahma. One story tells that when Brahma first made the universe, he realised that it was disordered and chaotic. So then he created knowledge to bring order and beauty. Sarasvati – the physical form of knowledge – came from his mouth and immediately she began telling Brahma how to make the sun, moon and stars. Together they created the oceans, the mountains and the changing seasons.

A stone figure of Sarasvati, India, 1100s

From the earliest tales (some over 2,000 years old), Sarasvati is connected with a powerful ancient river. In these stories the goddess took on the characteristics of a mighty flood of water, roaring with energy like a bull and snorting like a boar. She bursts down the sides of the mountains to meet the ocean and is full of life. Like a river that gives life to those that respect it, the goddess can provide everything from a new baby to the gift of knowledge.

TURNING HEADS

When Brahma first saw Sarasvati he was captivated by her beauty. He was embarrassed by how much he admired her and didn't want his sons to see him following her with his eyes. The goddess walked around Brahma while he struggled to stay still. As she walked to one side he longed to see her and so another face appeared. Then she moved behind him and again he produced another face at the back of his head. Scared by his attention, Sarasvati tried to escape by flying up into the air but a fourth head appeared on top of Brahma's head. And so Brahma is always shown with four heads because he simply had to enjoy the beauty of Sarasvati. Together they had a son – the first man, Manu. Sarasvati's role as mother and protector of mothers is another reason why she is so important.

SHAPING BELIEF

During Sarasvati's springtime festival in India where worshippers wear yellow, children are taught to write for the first time. People also pray to her for blessings on their books and musical instruments or before exams.

Sarasvati is sometimes described as a cow, nurturing worshippers with the milk of creativity, or as a river flowing with inspiration. So she is mother, river and wisdom all in one.

Hindus still consider rivers to be sacred, and bathing in the river Ganges, which flows from the Himalayan mountains to the sea, is an important ritual today. Water brings life, health, strength and purity, so Sarasvati's connection means she too can deliver these gifts. In art she is connected with the colour white, symbolising truth and light. She's often accompanied by other white things, like a royal goose and lotus flowers.

Sarasvati is an incredibly beautiful goddess with four arms – two play her musical instrument, the veena, while the others hold a book of ancient Hindu stories and beads for praying. Sarasvati is elegant, wise and complex and she inspires Hindus across the world to create, think and write.

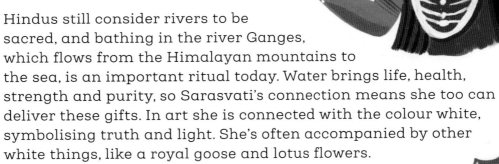

TARA
Buddhist Mother of Compassion and Wisdom

BORN FROM TEARS

Tara is one of the most important goddesses in Buddhism and is adored across the world. She's the focus for meditation, helping people to understand qualities like compassion, emptiness and loving kindness. With different names and in different ways she is honoured as bringing love, guidance and support to humanity.

Tara was born from the tears of Avalokiteshvara – 'Lord who gazes down at the world'. In one story, Avalokiteshvara was sitting peacefully at the top of the Red Hill, but down on the Plain of Milk he saw hundreds of people suffering thirst and hunger. He was so sad to hear their calls for help, and the sorrows of the world overwhelmed him. He began to cry uncontrollably, weeping a lake of tears. In the centre of the lake a lotus flower bloomed and Tara emerged. She was born from empathy and sorrow.

ETERNALLY FEMALE

There is another story about Tara's origins, which says she was first an ancient princess called Yeshe Dawa, which means 'Wise Moon'. Wise Moon had achieved great wisdom through the Buddhist teachings of Tonyo Drupa. She was close to enlightenment and had the chance to be reborn as a Buddha when a monk said to her that in order to reach her true potential, she should pray to be reborn as a man. Wise Moon turned on the monk, replying that, "Only weak-minded people see gender as a barrier in reaching enlightenment."

She then made a promise for the future and said, "It's true that very few have wanted to help humans towards enlightenment in a woman's form. I developed my wisdom as a woman. So in each of my lifetimes along the path I promise to be reborn as a woman." After this she entered a state of meditation for ten million years and over these years saved ten million souls. She has returned time and time again as a woman to help people in need.

SHAPING BELIEF

Tara can take different forms depending on what people need from her. These forms have different names and phrases that worshippers use to gain Tara's help. She is the 'North Star', leading the way and helping people navigate the stormy waters of self-doubt or anxiety. In one prayer she is serenity, patience and meditation, while in another she can trample worlds underfoot and has the strength to summon all power to her.

The goddess is also shown in different colours. As Green Tara she can protect against all the things that scare you most, banishing bad dreams and fears. As White Tara she can bring long life, get rid of illness and keep you calm. She's often shown sat on her lotus flower, cross-legged with one foot facing forward as if she is ready to spring into action.

Those who pray to the goddess often use a mantra that can be loosely translated as 'Om! Hail to Tara (in her roles as a saviouress)!' The fact that Tara insisted on remaining true to her identity is something women and girls everywhere can hold on to. She remains a source of strength and inspiration to women, and men, across the world.

A copper figure of Tara, Nepal, 1000–1200

CHANG'E

Chinese Goddess of the Moon

A HEROIC HUSBAND

Chang'e is a very popular goddess in China, who is often shown in the moon or holding the moon. Stories say that she is the goddess who took the elixir of eternal life to save it being stolen from her husband. She escaped to the moon, with a magic rabbit as her only companion. The rabbit constantly pounds the elixir of life in a pestle and mortar to keep the goddess with it for eternity.

A stone statue of Chang'e in Kuan Yin Temple, Malaysia

Before she flew up to the moon, Chang'e's husband was the greatest archer of all time, Hou Yi. In one famous story, ten suns, who were the grandchildren of the Jade Emperor, orbited the sky and scorched the earth. Imagine multiplying the heat of the sun ten times!

This led to complete chaos: crops burned, people collapsed, and, seeing the world in disorder, many dark and evil creatures began to roam. Hou Yi begged the Jade Emperor to let him deal with the suns, but the Emperor loved his grandchildren and did not want them to be shot. The Emperor called out to the suns, but they were laughing so loudly they couldn't hear him. Eventually the Emperor gave Hou Yi permission to save humankind. He fired nine arrows from his powerful bow and nine suns fell from the sky.

DRINKING ETERNAL LIFE

As a reward for saving humankind, the Jade Emperor's wife gave Hou Yi a magic potion in a bottle. By drinking it he could become immortal and go to the heavenly palace as a god. He was worried, though, because he knew this would mean leaving his beloved wife Chang'e behind. So Hou Yi hid the bottle.

Then, one day, his apprentice broke into their home and tried to force Chang'e to give the potion to him. She refused. She knew the young man couldn't be trusted with the gift of eternal life, so Chang'e decided to swallow the contents of the bottle herself.

The potion turned Chang'e into a goddess and as she floated up towards the heavens, she chose the moon as her home. That way she could still be close to the husband she loved so much.

When he discovered that Chang'e had drunk the elixir, Hou Yi thought she had betrayed him and acted as a thief. Hou Yi aimed an arrow at the moon but could not bring himself to shoot his wife. Eventually his anger calmed and he wanted to see Chang'e again. To tempt her home he left her favourite desserts out at night-time and this tradition continues today as part of the Mid-Autumn Festival.

SHAPING BELIEF

Every year on the fifteenth day of the eighth lunar month, people offer up sweet treats and moon-shaped cakes in memory of Chang'e and to celebrate the large harvest moon. This is known as Zhongqui Jie, or the Mid-Autumn Festival. People believe the offerings will bring good luck and happiness for the year. They also exchange moon cakes with friends and neighbours, and look up at the moon to see if they can see the goddess's outline on its surface.

While Chang'e is connected with the moon, she does not represent it. She lives on it as an immortal woman and it's this connection that is celebrated today. In fact, the Chinese Lunar Exploration Programme, which is trying to get a better understanding of the surface of the moon, is even named Chang'e, after the goddess.

PTE SAN WIN

Sacred Prophet of the Lakota

THE WHITE BUFFALO

The story of Pte San Win was probably first told by the Native American Lakota people over 2,000 years ago, and it's still just as important today. The miraculous tale of a white buffalo appearing in the desert connects them to the natural world, but it also gives the Lakota an origin story in which men and women show respect for one another. Pte San Win's knowledge gave the Lakota people their rules and rituals, but also provided love and protection, which will stay with them forever.

Most versions of Pte San Win's story start in a flat desert landscape with nothing anywhere on the horizon. Two men were hunting to provide food for their starving people. They noticed a small dot far away in the distance, which got larger as it came closer.

Soon the outline of a beautiful woman was clear. Most of her body was covered by waves of long dark hair, shrouding her like a cloak. Her outline glowed with hot light and she carried a bundle in her hands. The two men were entranced. One recognised her immediately for what she was – a Wakan, or Mystery. He turned his eyes away from her out of respect, while the other man kept on staring. He was full of desire and approached Pte San Win, trying to embrace her. But as he touched her skin, he instantly disappeared. At the feet of the beautiful woman lay a pile of bones and dust.

The surviving man was terrified and awestruck. Pte San Win told him that she had something important for his people. He must run to the village and prepare for her arrival by setting up a sacred tent with a buffalo skull at the centre. The people should wait patiently for her there.

Eventually a perfectly white young buffalo appeared. Rolling on the ground four times, it changed colour from white to black, then yellow to red. After the final turn, the buffalo transformed into the beautiful woman, who stood up and shone with the sun. She told the people that Wakan Tanka, the Great Mystery, had sent her to help them. She showed them a pipe and said that its smoke would take their prayers up to the Great Mystery and they would receive all they needed.

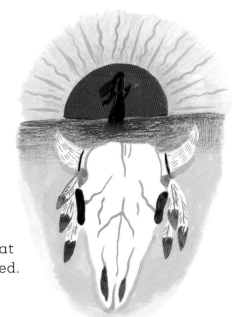

"I WILL SEE YOU AGAIN"

Pte San Win spoke with the people for four days and gave them all her wisdom. She told them that she exists across time and will return every generation to help in times of hardship. Her parting words were "I will see you again", and as she transformed back into a white buffalo, a great buffalo herd arrived on the plain.

A smoking pipe carved in the shape of buffalo, USA, 1860

Pte San Win had provided buffalo so the people would never go hungry or be cold. They would have food from their meat, clothes and tents from their skins and could make tools from their bones. Her visit had also set the people on a path to knowledge and understanding, as she nourished them in body, spirit, mind and heart.

SHAPING BELIEF

Pte San Win established the seven rites of the Lakota, which are still important today. These include the vision quest, ghost-keeping ceremony, sun dance and rituals for boys and girls entering adulthood. With these she provided the ties that still bind communities together.

The Lakota honour Pte San Win through the sacred ceremonies that she taught them, which included the pipe that she taught them to use. To them, white buffalos are the most sacred living animal. They are extremely rare, so whenever one is born, it can be seen as a sign that prayers are being answered. It also brings hope that Pte San Win may soon return.

LAKSHMI

Hindu Goddess of Wealth and Fortune

AWESOME POWER

Lakshmi controls wealth, fortune, love and beauty and is one of the most popular Hindu goddesses. Her name means 'she who leads you to your goals'. If you are loyal to her, but also work hard to be brave and virtuous, you will be rewarded. Also known as Shri-Lakshmi, she is worshipped during the major Hindu festival of light Diwali.

In Hinduism, female goddesses often use their energy to activate a male god's power, so Lakshmi is also important as the wife and balance of the main Hindu god, Vishnu. But she is also powerful in her own right as an awe-inspiring queenly goddess. She banishes her sister, Alakshmi, who is her opposite in every way, representing misfortune, poverty, hunger and thirst.

The first part of her name, Shri, is mentioned in the very earliest *Vedic* texts – the oldest sacred texts of Hinduism. Shri is awesomeness, shining power and magnificence. Think of a radiant, rich, all-powerful ruler and that is what Shri looks like. In one very famous story, we learn how the goddess got her joint name of Shri-Lakshmi, and how the universe simply cannot exist without this most important goddess.

THE MILKY OCEAN

Lakshmi first appeared in the Hindu story of the churning of the Milky Ocean. It began as the gods continued to struggle in battles against demonic forces. To defeat the demons they needed an elixir of immortality, but it was hidden deep in the ocean. The gods took the top of Mount Mandara to use as a churning stick, and held the tail of the serpent Vasuki for a rope. To steady them, Vishnu transformed into a tortoise, balancing the stick on his back.

Together the gods churned the ocean for 1,000 years and many wonderful gifts were brought up from its depths, including the moon, the cow of plenty and a shower of gemstones. Lakshmi emerged on top of a lotus flower, bringing balance and harmony. At the same time the elixir of immortality finally appeared. The gods gained eternal life and Lakshmi gave humans the hope of love and beauty.

SHAPING BELIEF

It might not sound like the greatest aspect of a goddess, but in some communities Lakshmi is worshipped in cow dung. Why? Well, this is the fertiliser that feeds the earth. With it crops can grow, families can be fed and the rich soil can give everyone life. One text says her son is called Kardama, which means 'mud', so she gave birth to the mysterious power of the earth. Her life-giving powers also explain why Lakshmi is often shown floating on a lotus flower. Just like the goddess, these flowers can grow in murky waters, yet blossom with life and colour.

Lakshmi appears across time in many different forms, loyally accompanying her husband Vishnu whenever he takes on a different form. This is why you'll often see images of her massaging the god's feet – the ultimate devoted companion.

But she is not always docile and passive. She can also be fickle, leaving her worshippers if they do not follow her guidance, and allowing her sister, Alakshmi, to take away a family's riches. Some people even say her changeable nature means pictures of her are constantly moving.

An image of Lakshmi is hung in houses to encourage good fortune and keep poverty away. She shines golden bright with four arms, each of which represents aspects of human existence: living honourably, enjoying life, having purpose and seeking enlightenment. Friday is Lakshmi's sacred day and devout Hindus worship her each week, with extra celebrations throughout the year. As bringer of light, beauty, riches and love, she is a powerful goddess, who can help you reach your goals in life.

A bronze figure of Lakshmi, India, about 1000

POPA MEDAW

Burmese Flower-eating Ogress

SACRED MOUNTAIN

In Myanmar (also known as Burma), Buddhism has blended with local traditions to honour a set of spirits known as *nats*. These were people who suffered unfair, painful or violent deaths, and so remain in the spirit world, unable to be reborn. One of the most important of the nats is Popa Medaw – an ogress who lived in the mountain of flowers.

Mount Popa is the home of the nats – it's a little bit like Mount Olympus for the Greek gods – and Popa Medaw is the spirit of the mountain. Temples and shrines to honour the nats sit on the top of Mount Popa, and pilgrims visit throughout the year to join in festivals and leave offerings for the spirits.

Mount Popa is an extinct volcano and it's often covered with beautiful and medicinal flowers. Almost 1,000 years ago, during the reign of King Anawrahta, a girl called Mei Wunna lived on the side of the mountain. She is described as an ogress, but rather than eating flesh, like other ogres, Mei Wunna only ate fruit and flowers.

Anawrahta was the first historic king of Myanmar and five of his followers were so loyal, brave and bold, he treated them like his sons.

They each had their own special skill. One of the five followers, called Byatta, had developed supernatural powers as a result of eating the flesh of an alchemist who possessed the elixir of life. Every day the king ordered Byatta to ride 30 miles to collect wild flowers from Mount Popa and present them at court. He was fast and strong so he was able to race to the mountain.

PAINFUL LOVE

While searching for the most beautiful blooms he discovered Mei Wunna and instantly fell in love. Statues of Popa Medaw show her with a pretty female face below – the one those who love her see – and an ogress's head above. Byatta, himself possessed of unusual powers, saw only the ogress's beauty. Mei Wunna fell in love with the brave, magical, strong man from the king's court and soon she gave birth to two boys. Sadly her happiness didn't last long.

A carved wooden figure of Popa Medaw, Burma, 2014

Byatta was killed for not showing due respect to the king and Mei Wunna grieved for him on the side of Mount Popa. The loss of her lover broke Mei Wunna's heart. She died full of sadness and grief, so was destined to remain part of the spirit world forever.

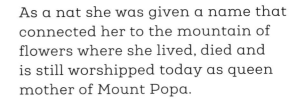

As a nat she was given a name that connected her to the mountain of flowers where she lived, died and is still worshipped today as queen mother of Mount Popa.

After her death, the king asked her two sons to serve him. They became great warriors but also died tragic deaths so they too are honoured as nats. The story goes that when they wouldn't help the king build a shrine they were killed on the spot. But as the king was about to leave court, the brothers appeared to him in spirit form. He realised they had remained in the world as nats, so he built them their own temple. Popa Medaw is often shown with two tigers that represent her sons, which shows that the family has never been forgotten.

SHAPING BELIEF

Today people honour Popa Medaw with offerings and she can also be contacted through a nat *kadaw*, or spirit medium, who channels and communicates with her. There are festivals to the nats on Mount Popa in June and November each year.

As the spirit who dwells in the most sacred mountain, Popa Medaw continues to provide protection for the people of Myanmar.

SEDNA

Inuit Mother of the Sea and All its Creatures

A NASTY TRICK

Sedna, the Mother of the Sea, who is also known as Nuliayuk or Taluliyuk, is honoured by the Inuit who live in northern Arctic lands. They depend on seals, walruses and whales to survive, and Sedna's amazing story explains where these sea creatures very first came from.

Yet Sedna can also cause trouble as she sometimes hides the animals the Inuit hunt, brings about cruel storms and sends sickness among people.

There are many different versions of her stories, but in Greenland they believe Sedna was a beautiful young woman who lived with her father, Isarrataitsoq. All the local men wanted to marry her, but Sedna turned down offers again and again. That was until one day a very handsome man came to promise her a wonderful new home. This time Sedna was charmed and decided to say yes. But everything was not quite as it seemed.

Her handsome new husband turned out to be a terrible bird spirit in disguise, and she soon realised his house in the ocean was not wonderful at all – it was cold and damp. She was always hungry and she had to wrap herself up in slimy fish skins to keep warm. She cried out across the freezing seas for her father.

An Inuit stone figure of Sedna, Canada

CREATOR OF SEA CREATURES

Isarrataitsoq came to the rescue and when he discovered how Sedna's new husband had tricked her, he tried to take her home in his kayak. Furious at his wife's escape, the angry bird spirit followed them. He whipped up the sea with his wings, creating a violent storm, and then he attacked the boat. In a panic Sedna's father cruelly threw her into the icy water to lighten the load. She clung to the side of the boat while the storm raged and the waters whirled around her.

When Sedna's husband did not stop his ferocious attack, Isarrataitsoq tried to peel his daughter's fingers from the edge of the boat. She gripped on so tightly, he took his paddle and hit Sedna's clasped hands instead. The first blow cracked her fingertips. They fell into the sea and transformed into a seal. But still, she clung on. Then he lashed out again and this time the rest of her fingers splashed into the water and turned into a walrus.

Isarrataitsoq's last blow cut Sedna's hands off completely and as she fell backwards from the boat, her hands touched the sea and they became a whale. She sank to the bottom of the ocean, her long black hair wrapping around her in the water. Here Sedna became mother of the underwater kingdom alongside all the creatures that had come from her own body.

SHAPING BELIEF

Sedna is an incredibly important figure for the Inuit because she holds the sea creatures tangled in her hair. She can keep families alive with her kindness when she decides to release animals for hunting or, when she is angry, she can hold on to them, causing people to starve. During times of hunger, spiritual leaders perform complicated rituals and special chants where they dive to Sedna's home at the bottom of the ocean, comb her long black hair, and ask for help. They believe that Sedna will only let the animals go when a shaman visits or she is given offerings. As summer arrives, the Inuit sing songs to her and when the first sea mammals are caught in the hunt they are cut into parts and placed in the water as gifts. As Mother of the Sea, she has great power over life and death and is essential to the Inuit of the Arctic north.

ITZPAPALOTL

Aztec Skeleton Warrior and Butterfly Goddess

OBSIDIAN WINGS

The Aztec goddess Itzpapalotl is constantly changing her appearance. She can either look like a beautiful young woman or a terrifying winged skeleton. At the end of her fingers are sharp jaguar claws while her feet have eagle talons. She also has razor-like blades on the tips of her wings, which she can use to tear apart her enemies.

She is a powerful warrior woman connected with life and death. Her name means 'Obsidian Butterfly'. Obsidian is a type of volcanic glass that was incredibly precious to the Aztecs. Gazing into its shiny black surface allowed you to move between past, present and future, speak with spirits and gain protection against evil. Itzpapalotl's connection with obsidian meant she had all these powers too.

Her wings could be black and leathery, like a bat's, or colourful like a butterfly's. Flying creatures represented the soul flitting between earth and heaven. They're also connected with reincarnation, bringing new life after death. Think of the life cycle of a butterfly – they seem to die when they have changed from a caterpillar into a chrysalis, but emerge alive and much more beautiful than before. In fact, carvings of butterflies were often put into graves by the Aztecs, perhaps calling on Itzpapalotl to take the dead to her peaceful paradise.

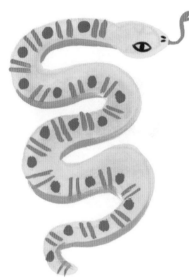

RULER OF PARADISE

Itzpapalotl rules over the paradise kingdom of Tamoanchan. Aztecs believed that this was where all humans were made. Here the blood from sacrifices and the ground-down bones from the realm of the dead are transformed into new life. It's also where children that die young are kept safe. A tree in the centre of the kingdom even drips milk to keep babies full and happy.

All time is present in Tamoanchan and the gods are connected to humankind. As ruler of this magical kingdom, Itzpapalotl is known as a creator goddess. She is also a shape-shifter and master of disguise. In one story, she dressed as a lady of the Aztec court, covering her face in white powder to change her appearance. She threw on her invisibility cloak so she could move unseen among humans and hear their stories.

In another myth she transforms herself again. After a terrible battle Itzpapalotl goes from a two-headed female deer to a beautiful woman. She wanted to charm one of the Cloud Snakes – a powerful spirit – and tried to persuade him to drink a potion. But it was a trick and the potion was actually blood.

Full of the drink, the Cloud Snake lay down, but instead of kissing him Iztpapalotl killed him. She is a goddess who uses her bare hands to defeat her enemies.

SHAPING BELIEF

Itzpapalotl has many roles and takes on many forms. She is one of the 'Divine Women', who look after those that give birth. The Aztecs saw childbirth as a powerful battle between life and death, so these women were honoured as great warriors. She is also queen of the Tzitzimime – the army of skeleton star demons. At the end of the present age the Aztecs believed that the Tzitzimime, led by Itzpapalotl, would come to earth in the form of horrifying beasts and devour all humans.

While this might make her seem scary, Itzpapalotl is a powerful protector of women and children. Love comes with pain, healing with sickness, and it's this balance of the positive and negative that she represents. She has the lightness of a floating butterfly but the power of a jaguar, and to the Aztecs she was a vital goddess who ruled over the role of women as creators of new life.

An Aztec ceramic butterfly stamp, Mexico, 1300–1550

BADB CATHA
Irish War Goddess and Battle Crow

HAG, CROW OR FAIRY

Badb (pronounced 'Bav') Catha is most at home among the howl, clash and noise of battle. Feared as the boldest of warriors, she could turn the tide of war and bring victory to whoever was on her side. The battlefield was even known as 'the garden of Badb'. In Irish mythology Badb Catha has two sisters and together they are a triple goddess known as 'The Morrigan' or 'Phantom Queen'.

Like a crow, Badb flies over the battlefield. She can kill warriors in a heartbeat and if you heard her wail on the winds, you would know that death was coming. She is a *bean-sidhe*, similar to a banshee – a fairy-woman whose cry shows that someone important is about to die.

In one story, Badb Catha appears as an old hag and washes the chariot of the hero Cormac Condloinges. This simple act was, in fact, a terrible omen, as seeing the goddess meant that the hero was going to die. She's the last person you'd want to lay eyes on before going into battle! Of the three sisters Badb is most often shown as an old haggard lady with witch-like powers to predict the future. But that doesn't mean she can't also fight furiously.

BOLD IN BATTLE

Many of Badb's stories are wrapped up with the myths of the history of Ireland. Medieval legends told of waves of invasions, with Badb's people, the Tuatha De Danann or 'Folk of the Goddess Danu', fighting against another group, the Fir Bolg. According to these stories, humans were the last group to arrive in Ireland, and the Tuatha De Danaan eventually became the fairy-folk, living in a supernatural realm alongside humans. Some people in Ireland still fear and honour the fairies today.

Badb played an important role in the battles between the Fir Bolg and the Tuatha De Danaan. With her sisters she made a thick cloud of mist cover the soldiers and brought a rain of fire down on the enemy. The goddesses stirred up a howl of noise and confusion and, in the chaos, the warriors had no rest for three days and three nights. Exhausted, the Fir Bolg were finally defeated.

Badb also battled against a more ancient enemy known as the Formorians. These were monstrous, foul beings who lived under the sea or deep in the earth. They represent darkness, death and drought. By destroying these creatures, Badb wiped out these evil forces. At the moment of victory the goddess sang a powerful song representing hope and celebrating a future full of joy. For her role in defeating evil she can be seen as full of power and positivity.

An iron sword, Roman, AD 200–300

SHAPING BELIEF

Badb Catha is still feared and honoured as one of the fairy-folk. Not the sweet, harmless fairies we might be used to, though. These are the magical Tuatha de Danaan, who are influential and secretive. You should never insult them and should give them offerings, like sharing whatever you are drinking.

It is a good idea to keep Badb Catha on your side. The image of a shrieking battle crow, causing chaos among soldiers, can make Badb seem scary, but she also protects rulers, tells the future and provides help for those that need it. If you're good to her, she will be good to you.

OSHUN

River Spirit of the Yoruba People

QUEEN AND CREATOR

Oshun is one of the most powerful orisha – spirits that order human existence and life on earth. She's honoured by followers of the Yoruba religion in West Africa and has also been reimagined and transformed in Cuba, Brazil and USA. This is because when enslaved people from Africa arrived in the Americas during the transatlantic slave trade, they carried their beliefs and the orisha, including Oshun, with them.

In the Yoruba religion Oshun is the source of all good things. She is very strong physically but can also get what she wants through her powers of persuasion. A loving creation orisha who protects, nurtures and supports, Oshun can also turn her powers against people. The river Osun in Nigeria is said to be the liquid body of the goddess and the source of survival for the people around it. Like the river, Oshun can give life and take it away.

At the beginning of time Oshun was the only woman among the male orisha. They had all tried to bring life to earth but kept failing. Eventually they handed power over to Oshun and she gracefully summoned her river. Life flowed into everything the water touched. But when Oshun was disappointed by her followers, she flooded the earth in anger, only letting the waters retreat when she had finally calmed down. She promised the Yoruba people that they could safely live alongside her river if they always honoured her faithfully.

THE KNIFE AND THE FAN

While Oshun is the cooling waters that are needed for life to flourish, in contrast, the most important male orisha, Ogun, creates and transforms through the white heat of iron and technology. He is god of blacksmithing and allowed the other orishas to enter earth by clearing a path with his huge metal axe. Oshun is a good balance for Ogun. If you think about how metal is made, you need flaming heat, but you also need cooling water to bring the molten material back to solid form. There is no life without Oshun, as her water heals, cools and feeds people.

A Yoruba wooden female figure, Nigeria, about 1950

Oshun is also a warrior and queen, showing that women can rule with strength. She is often seen holding a brass fan to bring cooling air in one hand, as well as a weapon – the brass sword or cutlass – which she uses to defend and protect her people.

SHAPING BELIEF

Oshun is still worshipped by many people across the world. Her followers ask her for help particularly if they are struggling to have children. In times of drought, Oshun can provide water and she is usually shown as a kind and generous spirit, ready to help those in need.

Her sacred colour is yellow and images often show her draped in golden cloth with a beaded crown and brass necklaces and bracelets. In Nigeria, there is a state and a river named Osun after her, as well as a sacred grove that is now protected as a World Heritage site. For two weeks in August people come together on the banks of the river and celebrate the goddess with dancing, drumming and singing. Oshun is an orisha who shows the many ways women can wield power and her goodness is balanced by her strength.

PELE
Hawaiian Goddess of Volcanoes, Fire and Lava

GODDESS OF MOUNTAINS

Pele, the volcanic *akua* (or goddess) of the Hawaiian islands, existed even before people had settled there around AD 900. Their storytelling traditions, passed down from generation to generation, describe heroes and gods. But others tell how the remarkable islands in the middle of the Pacific Ocean were formed. At the heart of these stories we find the goddess Pele. She probably started life as a fire goddess, but in Hawai'i she is bound to the active volcanoes that continue to shape the pattern of people's lives.

Pele's home is a sacred volcano called Kilauea and she lives in a crater at its very heart. Kilauea emerged from the sea tens of thousands of years ago and still erupts regularly, spewing lava across the south of Hawai'i island, causing devastation and laying the ground for regrowth. Like the volcanic mountains, Pele is beautiful and unpredictable, destructive and powerful.

A wooden female figure made by Tom Pico, Hawaiian Islands, 2001

In one story, Pele is descended from Papa (earth mother) and Wakea (sky father). Pele also has a lot of brothers and sisters, but two of the most important are Hi'iaka and Namaka. Battles with her siblings not only show the powerful aspects of Pele's personality, but also her playful and affectionate side.

Like the Hawaiian people who continue to honour her, Pele first arrived on the islands by travelling across the ocean. Different stories say how she reached Hawai'i and one tells of a furious fire battle between Pele and her sister. As she journeyed across the oceans Pele tried to make fires on each of the islands she landed on. But her sister chased her all the way, putting out her flames. In the end they fought, sister to sister, and Pele was killed. Her body melted into the mountains of Hawai'i and her spirit became the volcanic earth of the island.

Pele is believed to exist in the rocks and lava of the mountains. While destroying everything in her path, she leaves behind her hair and tears in remarkable pieces of volcanic glass.

LIFE, LOVE AND LAVA

Pele brings destruction but she also brings life. With each volcanic eruption, she gives birth to new lands for the Hawaiians of the future. Stories surrounding Pele also talk about her caring side. In one, her mother gave her an egg to look after. Eventually it hatches and the goddess inside becomes her sister Hi'iaka.

Pele loved her sister dearly but became jealous when Hi'iaka made a new best friend. Stories tell how Pele sent Hi'iaka to deliver a message to her lover, Lohiau. Thinking Lohiau had cheated on her with her sister when she didn't return home, Pele became more and more frustrated. As punishment, she sent a wave of lava down on to the home of Hi'iaka's best friend, turning her to stone.

When Hi'iaka returned and saw her friend dead she spitefully embraced Pele's lover and in fury the goddess poured lava over the two of them as well. Pele was devastated with sorrow and after a while realised she should bring all of them back to life. When Hi'iaka and Lohiau recovered they decided they did want to be together after all, so Pele's punishment was to watch her lover choose her sister.

SHAPING BELIEF

Pele is still incredibly important to the people of Hawai'i. They continue to honour her by offering their prayers, dances and gifts to the volcanoes themselves. The group of islands is known for a type of dance called the hula, which is used to honour Pele. Her mountains also continue to be protected and honoured sites.

Recently, as plans developed to build another huge telescope on top of Mauna Kea, the tallest volcano in the Hawaiian islands, they were disrupted by loud singing and dancing ceremonies and resistance of the *kia'i* – protectors of this important place. Goddess of volcanoes, fire and lava, Pele is not someone you'd ever want to anger!

SPIDER MOTHER

Native American Creator of Cures and Good Advice

THE GIFT OF WEAVING

Stories about the creator Spider Mother have been told for many centuries among the different tribes of south-west America. According to Navajo myths, where she is known as Na'ashjé'íí Asdzáá, the taller of the two towers at Spider Rock in Arizona, USA, is her home. Here the stone has turned white at the top where the bones of naughty children have dried in the sun. If a child misbehaved, Spider Mother would trap them high up in the sticky strings of her huge web.

But in most stories Spider Mother doesn't hurt people – she helps them. In one story, two important heros from Navajo mythology, the twins Tóbájíshchíní (Born for Water) and Naayéé'neizgháni (Monster Slayer) sought her help. In return for their respect, she gave them chants that would protect them and calm the anger of their enemies.

Navajo people highly value Spider Mother, because she taught the skill of weaving. She is so important that when Navajo women begin weaving threads, they smear spider webs on their hands to ensure a smooth process and to bless their work. Weaving used to be considered a sacred duty and women wove their prayers and blessings into their textiles, calling on Spider Mother for protection and guidance.

FIRE AND LIGHT

Another south-western tribe, the Hopi, also include Spider Mother in their stories. One tells how she gave humans their most important tool for survival – fire. The animals, birds and humans were all cold and lost in a dark, miserable world. They heard a rumour that in the east there was something called fire. They didn't know what it was, but wanted to see if it could bring some light to their world.

First an opossum stole a little piece of burning wood and hid it in his big, bushy tail. But the flames burned his fur to a crisp and the opossum ran away crying. Next, a buzzard flew over the fire, grabbed a burning ember and balanced it on its head. But again the poor bird didn't realise fire would burn and its feathers went up in smoke.

Finally, in her tiny spider form, Spider Mother said she would go. She used her long legs to mould a pot out of clay with a delicate lid on top. Tucking a tiny piece of burning wood inside the pot she wound her web round it and returned to the other creatures. The animals and birds fled, terrified of how it had harmed them. Only the humans wanted it, so Spider Mother gave them the gift of fire.

SHAPING BELIEF

Wise, kind and always ready to help, Spider Mother protects those that call out to her in need. As a human, she looks like a thoughtful old lady, but she can transform into a spider and go deep inside the earth to her lair. When people want advice, guidance or cures for sickness, Spider Mother crawls up from the ground to help them.

An eternal protector of humans, Spider Mother represents the webs that bind us all together. Her kindness helps everyone grow and, in a world where we're connected more strongly than ever, she remains a figure that can inspire all of us.

A postcard showing a Navajo woman weaving on a loom, Arizona USA, 1901

A seal showing Tiamat
as a dragon, Asia,
900–750 BC

TIAMAT

Babylonian Sea Dragon and Goddess of Salt Water

MOTHER OF GODS

Tiamat's ancient story is one of creation and new life, but also of revenge, war and death. She is a complex character – both mother of gods and creator of demons – and she is feared as well as honoured.

As goddess of the sea, she took Apsu, the god of underground fresh water, as her lover. The sea provides food and nourishment, while the fresh water in wells, rivers and lakes is safe to drink. Both types of water are necessary for life, and together Tiamat and Apsu created all the gods and goddesses of ancient Babylon.

As Tiamat gave birth to more and more children, the younger gods started to become a nuisance. They were noisy, disruptive and disrespectful. Tiamat tolerated their behaviour like a patient mother, whereas Apsu got cross with them. He told Tiamat that he was going to destroy this younger generation of gods. She ordered him not to, but Apsu feared that one of his children would try to take his place, so decided to carry out his plan anyway.

When the young gods heard of Apsu's plan, one of them – Tiamat and Apsu's son, Ea, the mischievous god of wisdom and magic – gave him a sleeping potion and killed him. Although she was still angry with her husband, Tiamat was even more enraged with the god who had caused his death – her own son!

BATTLING SEA DRAGON

Around this time, Ea also had a child who became the powerful god of storms, Marduk. Seemingly out of control, Marduk played with the wind, leaving chaos and destruction in his path. The other gods were frustrated by his actions and begged Tiamat to stop him. She wanted revenge for Apsu's death, and this was her chance. If she hurt Marduk, it would also punish her son Ea for killing her husband.

Tiamat created a vast army of monsters, led by her other son Kingu. To show that Kingu was now her favourite child, she gave him a powerful object – the 'Tablet of Destiny'.

Some of the other young gods were fearful that Tiamat was taking her new power too far. They tried to find a way to negotiate with her, but nothing worked. She would not back down. Eventually Marduk said he would fight the fierce goddess face to face. He only had one condition: that he would become chief of all the gods if he succeeded. The two locked in battle. Tiamat, in the form of a horrifying sea dragon, spat and lashed at Marduk with her tail.

To trap her, Marduk stirred up an evil wind and sent it crashing down. With the goddess unable to move, Marduk fired an arrow at her belly. It split her in half and as she fell apart, the god of storms knew he had won.

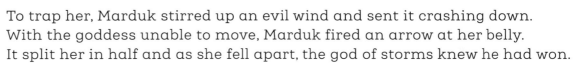

SHAPING BELIEF

An ancient text says that when Tiamat died, Marduk took parts of her body and used them to create the world. He hung up one half as the heavens and used the other half for the earth. Her eyes became rivers and her breasts became mountains. Her dragon's tail joined the earth to the heavens for all eternity, as the Milky Way. Tiamat's death also allowed Marduk to kill her other son, Kingu, take the Tablet of Destiny and mix his blood with soil to create humans.

Because Tiamat took the form of a terrifying sea dragon during the battle, she could be seen as a monstrous evil force. But, as mother of creation and a wife seeking revenge, she shows that a story can be more complex and interesting than simply 'good versus evil'.

AMATERASU

Japanese Sun Goddess and Mother of Emperors

BORN FROM HER FATHER'S EYE

Amaterasu is the oldest and most beloved daughter of the creator gods Izanagi and Izanami (see page 56–57). She is the goddess of the sun, which is shown on the flag of Japan. All emperors of Japan are said to be descended from her through her grandson Ninigi. This is how the imperial family claim the right to rule – it was given to them by the queen of heaven herself.

For followers of the Shinto religion, Amaterasu is the heart of Japanese spiritual life. As the sun moves across the sky and night follows day, so the goddess brings order, light and purity to humans. She lives in the High Plain of Heaven, Takamagahara, which is connected to earth by the Floating Bridge, Ame-no-ukihashi.

In one ancient story, Amaterasu's father, Izanagi, was bathing in the river. As he cleaned his left eye, the sun goddess Amaterasu was born. When Izanagi rubbed his right eye Tsukuyomi – god of the moon – appeared, and as Izanagi rubbed his nose, the storm god Susanoo appeared too. Amaterasu constantly fought with her new brother Susanoo and his crying and troublesome behaviour soon made their father cross. So Susanoo was sent away. Before leaving, angry and alone, he went to say goodbye to Amaterasu in her heavenly home.

A Shinto household altar made by Aokiya, Japan, 2016–2017

SISTER SUN, BROTHER MOON

Amaterasu was suspicious of her brother, so she dressed in men's armour to meet him at the gates of heaven. Wanting to prove himself, Susanoo suggested they take part in a trial to see who was more honourable. They each had to find an object, chew it up and spit it out. Amaterasu broke up her brother's sword and put it in her mouth. When she spat, three goddesses came out fully formed. Susanoo grabbed Amaterasu's necklace from her neck, chewed it to a pulp, and when he spat, a group of gods appeared. He claimed he had won, since he believed male gods were better than female goddesses. This was an insult to Amaterasu and all women.

Full of his victory, Susanoo went on a rampage through Amaterasu's kingdom. Like a toddler having a tantrum, he destroyed her throne and ruined her rice fields. The final straw came when Susanoo killed a horse – Amaterasu's sacred animal – and threw it at his sister's weaving loom, killing one of her maidens in the process. He was out of control!

Disgusted and fed up with her brother, Amaterasu went to hide in the Heavenly Rock Cave. As she shut herself away, all the light went out of the world.

Without the light and heat of the sun, everything began to die. The gods and goddesses, scared at what they were seeing, gathered outside Amaterasu's cave and tried to lure her out. Nothing would work. Eventually they begged the goddess of joy, Ama-no-Uzume, to start dancing. As everyone cheered and laughed, Amaterasu became curious. What could be so interesting out there? She peeked out and looked straight into a mirror that the gods had hung by the cave opening. She'd never seen her reflection before, so she wondered who this magnificent and powerful-looking goddess might be. Entranced by her own reflection, Amaterasu came out of the cave and light and warmth flooded back into the world.

SHAPING BELIEF

Amaterasu continues to be worshipped at the Grand Shrine of Ise, which is one of Japan's most holy sites, and is visited by thousands of pilgrims and tourists every year. The goddess is connected to three sacred objects that are still thought to be very powerful and, for the Japanese imperial family, are like their Crown Jewels. They are the Eight-Span Mirror, which lured Amaterasu from her cave, the Grand Jewel of the goddess and the Grass-Cutting Sword.

Amaterasu's story inspires people as it challenges traditional roles in society. Without her, the world is in darkness, so the way she can give or take away light and life shows that all women and girls have the potential to shine.

PAPATUANUKU

Maori Earth Goddess

MOTHER OF ALL CREATION

Have you ever wondered how the universe was made? We can imagine before history was written down, before humans appeared on the earth, before the planets were formed ... and what do we come to? A darkness. An emptiness. Yet a space bursting with the potential to generate life. For the Maori people of Aotearoa, New Zealand, this space is known as Te Po. From Te Po the first creators of life emerged. They were Papatuanuku (earth mother), and Ranginui (sky father).

It's impossible to tell the story of Papatuanuku without also writing about her partner, Ranginui. When the sky father and earth mother came together, they gave birth to the gods of all aspects of life on earth. The couple lay bound together, squeezing their children in the darkness between them, where they crawled around in a dark, damp space. But when Papatuanuku stretched up her arm they could see a beam of light shining. The gods wanted to live in this light, with space around them to explore, discover and create. So they began to plot ...

PAIN OF SEPARATION

The gods agreed they should push their parents apart. Ranginui could live distantly in the sky, while Papatuanuku would stay with them, nurture them and love them. However, as each one tried, one by one, they found it far too difficult. Then one son, the god of forests, Tane, attempted something different.

He turned himself upside down and used his legs to prise them apart. Along with him, all the trees turned so that their roots were in the soil and their leaves in the air. The wind god, Tawhiri, was so saddened at the separation of his parents that he rushed upwards to be with his father in the sky and continually moved between Ranginui and Papatuanuku, bringing howling storms to earth.

With Ranginui propped up in the sky, the two lovers cried for each other constantly. This frustrated the gods so they rolled Papatuanuku on to her front to face the Underworld – away from the sky. This didn't stop her pining for her love, though, and every morning the fields became full of her tears and rose towards Ranginui as mist. He also grieved, raining down enough tears to fill the seas and the rivers.

Although her children had caused her such pain, Papatuanuku kept loving them and created all the riches of the world to look after them. She continued to bring new life to the earth and it's said that when the goddess gave birth underwater, whole islands floated to the surface. One child remains beneath Papatuanuku though, trapped when she was rolled over – the god of earthquakes and volcanoes, Ruaumoko.

By controlling the movement of the earth, Ruaumoko brings the heat or the cold of his mother to the surface and controls the seasons. They stay close together and determine the patterns of life on earth.

SHAPING BELIEF

Papatuanuku continues to be seen as the physical and spiritual foundation of all life and is celebrated in Maori art and culture. In the Maori language, the word *whenua* means both 'land' and 'placenta' – this is the body part that grows inside the womb and feeds a baby during pregnancy. This shows that the role of land, and of women, to nourish and create new life comes together in the figure of the goddess Papatuanuku. Her beautiful love story and role as creator of all life means Papatuanuku has remained an influential goddess for centuries.

A stamp showing the legend of Papatuanuku and Ranginui, New Zealand, 1990

MAZU
Chinese Goddess of the Sea

TRAVELLING WITHOUT MOVING

What's interesting about Mazu is that she's the goddess form of a woman who really lived in Fuijan, China, 1,000 years ago. She's also known as 'Holy Mother in Heaven' and is the protector of all who take on the powerful sea, like fishermen, traders and travellers. Although she is known by many names, some say that prayers sent to Mazu (which means 'Granny' or 'Ancient Mother') reach her immediately.

The real woman behind the goddess was called Moniang or Lin Mo, which means 'the silent girl'. According to stories, she didn't cry at birth, or make a sound for the first years of her life. She had the gift of seeing the future and could visit a place in her mind, without having to physically travel there.

Once, the young girl was visited by a nun who had come from a temple many miles away. Moniang said to the nun, "Please bring me one of the flowers from the trees at your home." The nun was confused as there were no flowers on the trees when she had left. But Moniang insisted, "I know there are flowers because I've just been there and I've seen them. But I didn't want to pick one without your permission." When the nun returned home, sure enough, the trees were covered in blossom. Had Moniang actually travelled outside her body and seen the flowers?

GUARDIAN OF THE SEA

When Moniang's brothers left on a sea voyage one day, she fell into a deep trance and began crying and screaming for them. Her worried parents tried to bring her round and she was devastated to be woken, weeping inconsolably.

When her brothers finally returned to the harbour, they described what had happened while Moniang had been in a trance. Their ship was being battered by waves, yet they could see their sister in spirit form holding them steady in the water. As her parents had snapped her out of her vision, her calming image had vanished, and the eldest brother was thrown into the sea.

Moniang was so distraught that she couldn't save all her brothers that she vowed to remain single and in constant meditation for the rest of her life. She died very young but was then recognised as guardian of seafarers and, after death, she was respected as a goddess, Mazu. Despite the fact she never married or had children, in her goddess form Mazu is also worshipped as a protective figure for women who want to have a child.

Mazu continues to help those that need her. Over 300 years after the real woman, Moniang, died, an important man – the emperor's envoy, Zheng He – described how his ship was the only one in a huge fleet to survive a typhoon. He was afraid and unable to cross the fierce waters until Mazu appeared to him and guided the ship to safety. Honours were showered on her shrine as thanks.

SHAPING BELIEF

Many tales tell how Mazu has saved people from trouble at sea – from storms, pirates or even sea monsters. Her stories have sailed across the oceans with Chinese travellers for over 1,000 years. People from Fujian, on the south-east coast of China, migrated to Taiwan and took worship of Mazu with them, so she is especially honoured there where many people's lives centre on the sea and water.

A stone statue of Mazu at Vihara Satya Dharma, Bali

The goddess is still called upon to protect people from rough waters, with regular reports of visions and miracles. In 2016, her face was seen in the waves of a typhoon and this image spread around the world. Mazu is just as famous and well loved today as she was when the real Moniang was alive over a millennium ago.

GLOSSARY

ALTAR A holy table in a temple or church.

AMULET A small object or piece of jewellery carried to offer protection.

ASSYRIA A powerful kingdom that existed from the third millennium BC to around 600 BC, centred on the river Tigris, running through modern-day Iraq, Syria and Turkey.

AZTEC The Aztecs were people from what is now Mexico whose culture and religion flourished from around 1300–1600. The Aztec empire ended after being violently colonised by Spanish settlers in 1521.

BABYLONIA An ancient state based along the banks of the river Euphrates in the Middle East. Founded at the start of the second millennium BC, this ancient state was based along the banks of the river Euphrates in the Middle East. Its major city was Babylon, close to modern-day Baghdad in Iraq.

BIBLE A collection of religious texts sacred in Judaism, Islam and Christianity, seen as the revelations of one supreme being – God.

BUDDHISM Founded on the teaching of the fifth-century BC Indian Gautama Buddha, it spread across Asia to become the world's fourth-largest religion. The word *Buddha* means 'enlightened'.

CAPITOLINE TRIAD A group of three deities worshipped together in their main temple on the Capitoline Hill in Rome. They are Jupiter, god of sky and thunder, Juno, queen of the gods, and Minerva, goddess of wisdom.

CELTIC The Celts were a people bound together by language, religion and culture. Celtic territories stretched from the Black Sea, across Europe, down to Spain and across to the British Isles.

CENTURY One hundred years.

CHRISTIANITY The world's largest religion, founded on the life and teachings of Jesus Christ. Christians believe in one god and their sacred text is the Bible.

CIVILISATION From the Roman word for 'city', civilisations are places where humans live together and share knowledge and ideas.

COLONISATION The process of settling in a place that isn't your own. This usually involves forcing the indigenous population to live under your control.

CONTRADICTION Something that is opposite or different in meaning to something else.

CORPSE A dead human body.

DEITY A god, goddess or spiritual being.

ELIXIR Magical or medicinal potion.

EMPEROR The ruler in control of an empire.

EMPIRE A number of individual nations that are controlled by the government or ruler of a single country.

ENLIGHTENMENT The state of enlightenment is when a person has come to understand the truth about life. It is achieved through morality, meditation and wisdom.

ETERNITY An infinite or unending period of time.

FAMINE A period of starvation when food is in short supply.

HEBREW The language of the Jewish people, originating around Israel and Palestine.

HINDUISM The world's third-largest religion, Hinduism is an ancient Indian religion and way of life. Its roots go back many thousands of years and its four goals for human life are *dharma*, duty; *artha*, work; *kama*, passions; and *moksha*, enlightenment.

IMMORTAL Living forever, never dying.

IMPERIAL Relating to an empire or emperor.

INDIGENOUS A person, plant or object that originates in a particular place; native.

INJUSTICE A lack of fairness or justice.

ISLAM The religion of Muslims, Islam is the second-largest religion in the world. Muslims recognise one god, Allah. Islam was founded by the Arab prophet and leader Muhammad ibn Abdullah in the seventh century.

JUDAISM The religion of the Jewish people. Developed among the ancient Hebrews, Jewish people believe in one god who revealed himself to Abraham, Moses and the prophets.

LABYRINTH A complicated network of passages or paths where it is hard to find your way.

MANTRA The practice of repeating a word, phrase or sound to aid concentration and meditation.

MESOAMERICA A historic and cultural region stretching from central Mexico to northern Costa Rica. Before Columbus, ancient civilisations flourished here for thousands of years, including the Olmec, Aztecs and Mayans.

MESOPOTAMIA Meaning 'in between the rivers', Mesopotamia was the region between the Tigris and Euphrates rivers. This fertile area is now modern-day Iraq, Kuwait, Turkey and Syria.

MILLENNIUM One thousand years.

MINOAN Named after the legendary King Minos of Crete, the Minoans were a civilisation that thrived on the island from roughly 3000 to 1000 BC.

MORTAL Able to die.

MOURN To be sad at the death of someone.

MYTHOLOGY A collection of stories belonging to a particular religion or culture.

NORSE Referring to Norway specifically, but also the Scandinavian religion, language and culture of the medieval period.

NYMPH A mythological spirit of nature often imagined as a beautiful woman who lives in woods or rivers.

OTHERWORLD The spiritual realm or afterlife.

PAGAN A person holding religious beliefs that are based on a deep respect of nature. Pagan religions include ancient indigenous belief systems as well as modern Pagan communities.

PATRON SAINT A protective or guiding individual for a group or a place.

PHILOSOPHY The study of ideas about knowledge, right and wrong, and the value of things.

PILGRIM A person who journeys to a sacred place for religious reasons.

PROPHECY A prediction of what will happen in the future.

REBELLION The act of resisting authority and control by rising up against a government or leader.

REINCARNATION Rebirth of a soul in another body.

REVOLUTION A successful attempt by a large group of people to change the way their country is run by force.

RITUAL A religious ceremony in which a series of actions are performed in a certain order.

SACRED Connected with a god or goddess so deserving worship.

SACRIFICE Killing an animal or person as a gift to the gods and goddesses.

SHAKTISM A part of Hinduism that celebrates the eternal goddess as the source of all life, energy and power.

SHINTO A religion that developed in Japan in the eighth century AD. Shinto worshippers honour ancestors and nature spirits. They believe that sacred power (*kami*) flows through all living and non-living things.

SHRINE A special place where a particular god, goddess, saint or spirit is remembered, praised or honoured.

SLAVERY An enslaved person was considered property that could be bought, sold and owned.

SLAVIC People of Eastern Europe and Russia that speak a collection of related languages.

STRIFE Angry disagreement.

SUMERIA The earliest known civilisation in Mesopotamia, dating between 4500 and 1900 BC.

SYMBOL A thing that stands for something else.

TAOISM A Chinese spiritual tradition, originating around 400–301 BC, which stresses living in harmony with *Tao*, or the universe. Taoists believe in spiritual immortality, where the spirit of the body joins the universe after death.

TRANSATLANTIC SLAVE TRADE The enforced transportation of over ten million enslaved Africans across the Atlantic Ocean between 1500–1900.

UNDERWORLD The mythical land of the dead, often thought to be beneath the earth.

WICCA A form of modern paganism.

INDEX

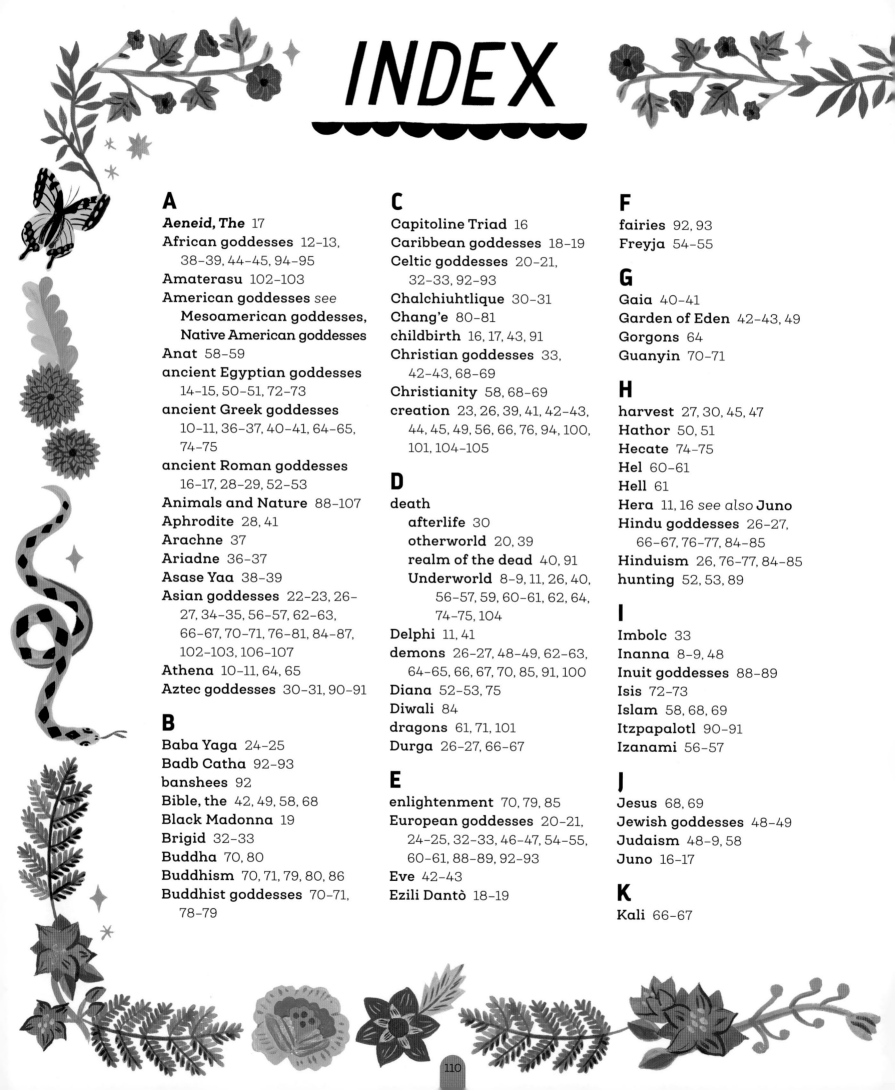

ACKNOWLEDGEMENTS

Thank you to Kate Wilson, Tina García, Victoria England, Leila Mauger and Rachel Kellehar at Nosy Crow for making the book happen, and to Jennie Roman for her excellent proofread. Thanks also to the knowledgeable and helpful curators and editorial team at the British Museum for all their hard work and brilliant ideas, especially Claudia Bloch, Kathleen Bloomfield, Lydia Cooper and Belinda Crerar. You have all been fantastic.